HARTZELL SPENCE

Happily Ever After

DRAWINGS BY
DEAN FAUSETT

Whittlesey House

McGRAW-HILL BOOK COMPANY, INC.
NEW YORK · LONDON · TORONTO

HAPPILY EVER AFTER

Published by Whittlesey House

A division of the McGraw-Hill Book Company, Inc.

PRINTED IN THE UNITED STATES OF AMERICA
BY THE HADDON CRAFTSMEN, SCRANTON, PA.

TO MARGARET

Happily Ever After

CHAPTER ONE

THE elevator operator surveyed me with some distaste. I had observed previously that he had taken upon himself the task of maintaining the tone of our apartment building by a haughty mien toward some of my writer and actor friends whose jackets and trousers did not match. But this was the first time he had ever leveled the full measure of his disapproval on me. During the long ride to the nineteenth floor his eyes encompassed the dainty details of his Chinese lacquer cage, then pointedly came to rest upon my two large bundles, roughly tied with rope. Clearly, this sort of debris belonged in the freight elevator.

I was too elated, however, to be made uncomfortable by this disparagement. Quite accidentally, during a trip to Washington, I had made a discovery which I was now hurrying to share with my wife.

To dramatize the situation, I did not, as usual, let myself into the apartment with my own key. I rang the doorbell, and then stood back, round-shouldered from the weight of my cargo.

Margaret did not rise to the occasion. Opening the door, she frowned at the sight of me.

"What on earth!" she exclaimed.

I carried my treasures into the living room.

"We've discussed this subject in the abstract for the last time," I said. "From now on, we act."

I am not by nature a practical joker, so Margaret could only conclude that army life, even in mid-town New York, had been too much for me. She associated nothing in our recent experience with these two monstrous, rope-tied bundles. Her cautious attitude did not, however, deflate my buoyancy.

"Write Guerrero," I told her, "and tell him we are on our way."

Now she understood.

For two years we had been talking about our friend Guerrero. We had met him in Argentina, and the encounter was a climactic moment in our lives. He had achieved everything we needed and did not possess: contentment, self-sufficiency, security. He was grounded in the rich heritage of past ages, yet he was as modern as tomorrow. And his philosophy, imbedded in the wisdom of accumulated centuries, in the natural world of animals and plants, and in a comforting belief in the goodness of God, gave him both mental and physical assurance. My mind associated him, for some reason, with the Inness painting "Peace and Plenty."

On December 7, 1941, Margaret and I had visited Guerrero on his *estancia*. In a carriage drawn by two horses in tandem we drove over thousands of acres of lush pasture and orchard which twenty years earlier had been a desert of uncontrollable sand dunes. Then we dined with our host in a house which had been erected on a promontory raised by the wind exactly where Guerrero had planned it to be. Until late in the day we sat, sated by meat, vegetables, and fruit, all grown on an erstwhile desert, listening to the tale of a man who had put the wind to work for him to reclaim land that now supported eight thousand cattle and forty families.

Guerrero had developed a technique for anchoring the shifting dunes. Starting with a hummock of grass pegged into the lee of a dune at the ocean's edge, he had turned the direction of the wind. As the grass grew higher and spread, the sand hill flattened out, filling a depression in front of it. Then seedling fir trees were set into the grass, further breaking the wind. In a decade, trees and grass covered thirty thousand fertile acres. Now, his knowledge perfected, Guerrero could create hills or level them, plant valleys or ridges wherever he chose along the waterfront. As we talked, he watched the wind at work not far away, piling up a very large hill on which he planned to erect a chapel overlooking the sea.

I was impressed. Guerrero enjoyed the good life, while the wind did his work. That was for me. I saw only the climax of thirty years of patient and expensive labor. I ignored Guerrero's disappointments, his costly experiments, his trials and errors. I saw only the wind, not the man, at work.

Even more than by what our host had done for the land, I was impressed by what the land had done for him. He sat composed, relaxed, looking much younger than his seventy years; alert, informed not only on husbandry but on his country, the world, and his own relation to the great universe.

Our interest was also intensified by the fact that at our age he had been, as we ourselves were at that moment, almost expatriate. He had traveled the world in search of something to ease his restlessness, only to return home at last unfulfilled. Then, he told us simply, he had gone one Sunday to walk a wasteland owned by his father along the ocean south of Buenos Aires. The wind whipped white sand across his face. Everywhere before him the dunes were on the march. For miles he paced the beach before he paused at a spot where in his childhood a summer cottage had stood. It was covered completely by the sand now, except for one rotting roof cornice that protruded from its grave. Once that house had been gay and meaningful, echoing the happiness of his childhood. Our host looked upon this desolation and saw in it himself.

"I did not like what I saw," he said, pinning Margaret and me in turn with a thrust of his sharp eyes. And I thought, "He is pointing a moral here. He is talking to us of ourselves, not of himself."

He was so right. Margaret and I were blowing about before the wind. In fact, our restlessness had drawn us together. Little more than a year earlier she had been working for a law firm in New York, I for a press association. Neither of us was any longer young, as youth measures years. At thirty-five I was gray-haired and fighting the first manifestation of middle age—resistance to change. Margaret was not quite thirty. Our jobs, while lucrative, were not fruitful except in material things. So we joined forces, married, and broke away together. There was no time to lose, for even then, with wars going on in Europe and Asia, and my age group registered for the draft, the world was closing its doors. There might be no permanence in our going, for the army would permit my absence from the country only for six-month intervals, renewable if there was no war, subject to immediate cancellation in an emergency. In defiance of the transiency of our passports, we sold most of our possessions and took off, determined henceforth to make our home where we found it.

For a year all was well. Then we began to be homesick. Yet we would not return to a life which involved office desks and a crowded city.

Then suddenly, listening to an Argentine rancher's story,

4

our world opened up. I looked at Margaret and she at me. Our host seemed to appreciate our discovery, for suddenly his reminiscence ended, and almost apologetically he said, "You have been very patient listening to an old man's reverie. Let's see what's in the news."

The news that came from his radio was the story of Pearl Harbor. We listened a moment in shocked silence. Guerrero said, "I suppose you'll be going home, now."

For almost anyone, caught in a foreign land by the outbreak of war, this question might have been answered simply, but for us there was no accurate response. We had no home, only a homeland. And Margaret and I knew at that moment that deep roots, firmly planted somewhere, are as essential to man as to a tree.

Ever since that day, we had been discussing, theoretically, the question of where to put down our roots. Geographically, it could be anywhere, since the writing by which I earn a living may be accomplished in any place where there is room to set up a typewriter. But undoubtedly there was one place, somewhere, which would contribute more to our happiness than any other.

What I desired, of course, was an Elysian field in which I could write and enjoy life while the wind did all the work. I fancied myself, in imagination, writing epic philosophical essays while gazing at contented cattle grazing on a neat horizon; or perhaps, in later years, now the mellow patriarch, elaborating to my many children from the leisure of a porch chair on the necessary elements of the good life.

My first military station was as editor of *Yank*, the army magazine, in New York. Margaret and I spent many evenings discussing the geographic locale of our future home. Our thoughts on balmy Argentina, we quickly turned away from the severe winter of New England. Further, we in-

5

sisted on being within a day's journey of New York's gaiety and opportunity, and this put a definite perimeter on our explorations.

Tucked away in the lower corner of this perimeter was a section of northern Virginia. It had a strong attraction in its gentle and leisurely climate, its appreciation of history and the good things of life. Here, we thought, we might settle down amid sunshine and honeysuckle, raise a big family— we thought nine children would be about right—and feel at one with the universe.

This speculation had produced nothing tangible. Then one day I had gone to Washington, and by chance happened into the Department of Agriculture. In the lobby were a thousand pamphlets—all free—concerning farming. At random I selected one, and read. Farming was so simple that there was really nothing to it. That's what the pamphlet said. You bought a mess of cattle and they supported you. If there was any little problem, a government bulletin was available to tell you exactly what to do.

Here was my Elysian field. Here, also, in the pamphlets, was the wind to do the work.

Enthusiastically I pounced on eight hundred of these pamphlets, covering every eventuality that might threaten to disrupt the good life, tied my literature into two bundles with a stout rope (also supplied free by the Department of Agriculture), and hurried home to share this remarkable discovery with Margaret.

Now, hastily in my excitement, I cut the rope on one of my bundles and flung the top two pamphlets at Margaret.

"It's so simple!" I exclaimed. "Why didn't we think of this before?"

Unfortunately, the two examples offered to my perplexed spouse happened to be No. 147, *House Ants;* and

6

No. 146, *Bedbugs*. The latter was on top. Margaret carefully scrutinized its title, and then, with equal care, turned to stare at me.

"Not those," I said quickly, and then, with more discrimination, selected two others. They were No. 840, *Farm Sheep Raising for Beginners*, and No. 1030, *Feeding Horses*.

"You see," I said, "you don't have to be born on a farm to be a farmer. You can just go by the books, and the books are free."

Margaret did some rummaging of her own at this point, and by the time I had arranged my pamphlets neatly on a book shelf, she had curled up in a chair with No. 1088, *Selecting a Farm*, and No. 1087, *Beautifying the Farmstead*.

Her action should have been an omen. I should have seen in what direction her interest turned. The phrase "a way of life" has two distinct meanings, one masculine, one feminine. For man, it is an outward view, toward the horizon; to woman it ends at the door of her home. A man, watching his cattle grazing in the field, sees them in terms of cents per pound of meat. A woman does not see them at all; she is looking over their heads toward a distant antique shop which has a great bargain that day in a Sheraton table. But this I had to learn.

Within a few days of my visit to Washington, Margaret was able to quote the booklet on selecting a farm. She even talked like a farmer, and began to stand like one, too, with her feet squarely set and wide apart.

"It says here," she tackled me one night after dinner, "that 'wise selection of a farm is vital to the success and satisfaction of farm life.' I think before you settle down with that very attractive No. 1045, *Laying Out Fields for Tractor Plowing*, we should have some idea what land you're going to plow."

7

This seemed to make sense, although at that moment I did not feel in the mood for discussion. The previous evening I had put down No. 218, *The Home Fruit Garden*, in the midst of planting some yellow peaches rich in vitamin A, and I wanted to get on with the job. Margaret's comment made me feel as though perhaps I was setting up my orchard on someone else's land.

We spent the entire evening, and several others, over No. 1088. On page nineteen there was a blank form for use in selecting a farm, against which it was advised to check any piece of real estate actually under consideration. This was so thorough that it inquired into drainage and whether the owner was able to transfer a sound title, as well as more obvious considerations of locale, fertility, water availability, and practicability of buildings. Margaret and I went over this check list on a dozen imaginary farms, and in the process agreed on the characteristics of our as yet nonexistent acres. The finger of the Department of Agriculture was heavily upon us, pointing the way.

We decided, finally, to look for a little place of about one hundred acres, to which Margaret would go when, inevitably, I was transferred from *Yank*, since no military station is ever permanent. She would be there alone—or as now seemed probable, with a baby—perhaps for some years if the war continued its unfavorable course. Our farm, therefore, must be in good repair and well fenced, with a house ready for occupancy. The residence must have at least one bathroom, electricity, telephone, and an electric pump. The fields and barns must be in such condition that we could begin to farm at once. (The pamphlet was firm about that.) The acreage must be small enough so that, with the aid of one paid hand, Margaret might run a few beef cattle while awaiting my return. The lawns and gardens must be small and easy to keep. We were not interested in serious farming to make money—although from the books I could see there was nothing to it—but we did want to be associated with the world of nature, to identify ourselves with the values that a man working the soil deems important. We sought a genial, leisurely background for a pleasant, happy way of life, one that would give us plenty of time to grow up with the children and enjoy each other. The pamphlet said, in this particular, that with modern machinery the days of farm drudgery were gone forever. At the same time, the farm must have the potential ingredients of self-sufficiency, a hedge against the possibility that, after the war, I might not be able to write again.

Now all we had to do was to find this place, and get on with pamphlet DS21, *Getting Established on the Land*. Like Noah's dove seeking land, Margaret ranged Virginia and the Carolinas seeking a homesite. The army, unrealistic in this as in so many matters, declined to let me accompany her. Margaret took with her the checklist from pamphlet 1088. But nothing seemed to measure up. Either she could not truthfully write "yes" in the blank space after the question "Are the fences in good repair?" or she was compelled to put a small, meek "no" in the space after "If you had to sell, would you find a ready buyer at the price you must pay?"

Meanwhile, comfortably at home, I worked my way through the basic knowledge of agriculture, and went on from animals and crops and pastures to No. 1564, *Farm Budgeting*, and No. 143, *Some Common Mushrooms and How to Know Them*. There was no doubt in my mind, this was going to be the life!

Only one of Margaret's prospects was I able to visit myself, and after seeing it I could only wonder why its owner had never taken advantage of all the government bulletins about farming. The place was an old Virginia farm without a fence on it, overgrown to poor quality third-growth pine, its sparse vegetation an eloquent duplicate of the photographs illustrating soil deficiencies in No. 194, *A Pasture Handbook*. Margaret was attracted to the place because it had once housed George Washington's grandmother, and the stable sheltered a collection of carriages of ancient design. She could visualize herself trotting to town in one of the old coaches behind a handsome pair, her nine children about her, and probably with several Dalmatians loping between the wheels as they had done on the Argentine *estancia*. What really caused us to reject the place, however, was not its unfruitful condition, but its inaccessibility. It was sixty miles from a railroad, and after a long wait in a station and a rough bus trip, we had no mettle to duplicate such a performance every time we went to New York. Moreover, the price seemed to be based more on Washington's grandmother than on the condition of the land.

We were especially disappointed at this outcome because Margaret was unable to continue her search. The arrival of the first of our projected nine children intervened. He was christened Lampert, after Margaret's brother who at that moment was in a hospital in North Africa after being wounded on the Italian front.

Naturally, the army could not overlook the fact that, during war, a couple was happily enjoying its first baby. I scarcely had a chance to read No. 1368, *How to Train a Pony*, when I received transfer papers to the Caribbean, and Margaret and the baby were left alone in New York.

Remembering the remarkable selling powers of Washington's grandmother upon Margaret, I was not sure I could trust her to select a home for us in my absence. Her inclination lay perilously toward the quaint, rather than what our pamphlets insisted was the practical. But I had no choice, for I had no idea how long I would be gone, and we were both anxious to begin the new life.

So I exerted what cautionary controls I could. I left Margaret a power of attorney to spend our nest egg to purchase the dream of one hundred acres if it materialized. She in turn promised to buy nothing which did not meet, in every respect, the Department of Agriculture's qualifications.

In retrospect, I realize that leaving my wife with a legal paper entrusting her with all my worldly goods might have altered our future radically. In my absence she might have bought a mink coat, a Cadillac convertible, and a nonexistent gold mine, and reduced us to such a state of penury that we should have abandoned all thoughts of a rural idyl.

All I can say, at this late date, is that I wish she had.

CHAPTER TWO

WHEN Lampert was a year old, I was transferred to the Air Staff and Margaret and I were reunited in a cigar-box housing development in Washington. Even more exciting than reunion was the proximity of the Pentagon Building to that section of the country in which we hoped eventually to settle down.

At such moments as we could find, we resumed our old search. We would take up headquarters in a hotel in Charlottesville over a week end, leave toddling Lampert riding up and down the elevator with its operator, who doubled as our baby sitter, and explore the countryside with a real estate agent. We found nothing. The shipshape places were too expensive, while those we could afford lacked some necessity, such as plumbing, or had something we did not want, such as termites.

We had about given up hope of finding anything that would fit our pamphlet-prescribed specifications when one day the agent wrote that he had found just the place. His description was convincing. By working ninety successive hours, I secured a free day and we rushed southward. If, as appeared likely, I was to be sent overseas soon, Margaret and Lampert might settle our home while I was gone. Margaret thought this a good idea, since nothing appeals more strongly to a woman than buying furniture while her husband is ten thousand miles away.

The real estate agent greeted us with word that the place he had described so attractively had just been sold; but agents always have another in reserve. We were really lucky, he said, because this other place would, if he knew us, fit us right down to the ground. It also had an imposing name: Gaston Hall.

Too weary from lack of sleep to protest, I took a nap while the salesman expounded at length to Margaret upon the rare opportunity that was ours, since by great good fortune, we were to have the first look at a property worth twice the money that was being asked for it.

What he showed us was scarcely a farm at all. The house was surrounded by seven hundred acres of land overgrown with weeds. Not a fence on the entire property was secure, not a building in repair. The entrance road was a quagmire. The price was low. It should have been.

Yet it was also imposing. The entrance cut through eight acres of what had once been a great lawn, lush with borders of neglected shrubs. On a knoll, facing a panorama of green fields that stretched miles away to the heights of the Blue Ridge mountains, sat a tremendous house of great architectural dignity. Four Jeffersonian capitals sustained a dormer sixty feet above ground, and sweeping away from a wrought-iron railed porch were two vast wings, each capped by a balustrade. Boxwood lined the carriage walk, and behind the house, framing it, acres of oak park merged at last with a hardwood forest. Restored to its former grandeur it would have been a setting for an English viscount, but it was clearly not for us.

The agent rang the front doorbell but there was no answer.

"Surely no one lives here," I said.

"Oh yes," I was informed. "An old fellow named Sheldon, but I think he's in Florida."

We climbed through a rear window, large rats scuttling before our feet, and stood, shocked and dejected, in what had once been an imposing entrance hall. Chinese grass-cloth hung in rotting streamers from the walls, a nest for thousands of silverfish. The floor was coated with used crankcase oil. In room after room this desolation of neglect was repeated. The electric wiring was obsolete, the plumbing antiquated, the paint long flaked from the woodwork. The furniture was equally shabby, the veneers peeling from cabinets and bureaus, and padding protruding from the silk covering of sofas.

Yet here again there had once been greatness. The architectural details were impeccable, the moldings and wood-work of a by-gone and richer era than our own. Nine fireplaces with marble mantels dominated the principal rooms. In the living room hung a chandelier of more than a thousand crystal pendants, and in the dining room dangled a rare, poured crystal chandelier. Every room was equipped with interior shutters of paneled pine. The mantel in the ballroom was ten feet tall, and so heavy it was supported by two Corinthian columns, and here there was also an orchestra balcony of heart oak.

Everywhere the rats retreated before us, moths and yellowjackets cluttered the windows, and every wall was damp and mildewed.

The real estate agent could not escape our unvoiced feeling of disbelief that such a shambles could exist at all, let alone be offered for sale. Quickly he took us back into the fresh sunlight, and tried to arouse our interest by showing us the two-bathhouse swimming pool (which had no bottom), the tennis court (which had no backstop wire), the

14

stable (which had no shingles left on the roof), and the barns (in whose windows every pane of glass was broken). The principal tenant house had once been an imposing building in its own right: it was a two-story colonial treasure built about 1797.

"It can easily be restored," the agent said.

"For about ten thousand dollars," I muttered.

At this point Lampert began to cry.

"You're right as rain, sonny," I said, and we headed back to Washington. We had not even bothered to look at the farm, for in a country property, so the book says, the house is always the last to be neglected. The land suffers first. Although I had seen that the fields were gently rolling, well-drained, and of easy cultivation, and apparently were well watered, the broom sedge had been waist high in the meadows, and a feeble wheat crop of about ten acres had looked to my pamphlet-instructed eye to be deficient in most of the vital minerals. Our last view of the farm had been of a building we had not been shown, over to the east, a large barn the roof of which was completely gone.

I had done without sleep for four nights in order to have an opportunity to inspect this derelict. I was not amused.

Margaret said nothing all the way home. This should have been a warning to me. Margaret sometimes talks without thinking, but when she is silent, her mind is spinning at a dangerous pace. I was too weary, however, to be wary. I had had enough of everything except sleep.

The following Sunday, the first in May, I found myself unexpectedly free of military duties. In addition, we had been issued a new gasoline ration, which suggested a short drive in the country.

"Let me drive, dear," Margaret said, "you look so tired."

You can guess where she went. At fifty miles an hour,

unconscious of wear and tear on our precious tires or the alarming dissipation of our gasoline supply, she sped to Orange County, as accurately as a homing pigeon. I have seen dogs and even cows find their way back over complicated routings, but never before had I witnessed this instinct at work in a human being. To all woman's other canny senses, add this one. In two hours we were before the sagging gates of Gaston Hall. But here, now, something had been added since our previous visit. A large sign proclaimed that on May 10 the place would be sold at public auction, "with all improvements."

"A medical laboratory should buy the place," I said after reading the sign. "The rats are already here."

Margaret was made of sterner stuff.

"If it's for sale, I guess we wouldn't be trespassing if we went in," she said. "Let's take another look, shall we, just for fun?"

So we turned into the lane. Dogwood, lilac, and redbud in full bloom now masked the desolation of the place, and clumps of unpruned forsythia screened dilapidation with brilliant yellow camouflage. Against the wings the osage orange was white with showers of snowy blossoms.

As we descended from our car before the house, certain evidences of neglect that had escaped us before now became apparent. Water marks on the brick betrayed leaky downspouts and perhaps a bad roof. There was a leprous scale of old paint on the porch rails. There were wide gaps between window frames and brick, and no sign of weather-stripping. I began to wonder why our real estate agent had not taken us into the basement. Investigation uncovered an ancient, wood-burning boiler connected to an antiquated steam heating plant, and three breaks in the foundation caused by the penetration of English ivy roots.

Margaret ignored all this. Impervious even to the cries of her baby, she stood successively in the door of each of the rooms, her big brown eyes flashing excitedly, her head cocked to one side. She squinted as though visualizing color combinations and groupings of furniture. She began to smile.

There was only one thing for me to do. Margaret had a deathly fear of termites. Surely in this old hulk of a mansion termites would be everywhere. I would find the evidence, call it to her attention, and we would leave Gaston Hall forever.

With determination I ripped plaster from the basement walls, laths from a third floor room, linoleum from a bathroom floor. I poked my pocketknife into seams in the woodwork and in timbers, joists, and floors. No termites. The house had indeed been solidly built. My zoological exploration gave me profound respect for the builders of that earlier day. They had obviously been craftsmen with pride in their work, men who would have felt it a personal dishonor to create something shoddy, for show only. I respected, too, the materials that had gone into this house: everything had been of the very best. Money had not been spent merely where it would catch the eye, in friezes, moldings, mantels, and sound oak floorings. The timbers, of heart oak and heart pine, were solid and secure. Like the reputation of the ancient architect, this house was meant to endure.

Musing thus, I left Margaret alone too long. When I returned to the hall, she had practically moved in. She was smiling and quiet, the most dangerous combination of storm signals in woman. She was not thinking of the fortune in repair bills that would be necessary to put the house in order. She had found a home, and she knew it.

17

In view of what was clearly going on in her mind, I was tempted to ask what had happened to our plan for a well-ordered hundred acres, but something told me the moment was not right for it. A woman will allow her husband to interrupt her conversation, but not her dreams.

I went out to explore the farm. The reconnaissance was not encouraging. The outbuildings were in worse condition than the house. The vegetable garden had a long rank of concrete cold frames, and rambler roses, about to bud, had taken possession of them. An ancient stallion grazed a patch of bluegrass near the dairy barn, the only evidence of livestock. Nor was there any farm equipment anywhere. The stable housed a shooting trap in good condition, but no other equipment. In a corner of an empty shed ominously rested a pile of hydrated lime. It had been there, I gathered, at least twenty years, and was probably a testament to the last program of soil nourishment the farm had known. I walked the banks of the streams throughout the property. Here at least was encouragement. The supply looked constant, and there was water available to every field. I removed a slab from a well, and threw in a stone, striking water almost immediately, and followed up this inquiry by tying a bolt to a piece of binder twine about a hundred feet long. The bolt did not touch bottom even when I paid out all the string. The ancients had indeed built with foresight. Like the well, every deteriorated detail was sound at heart. But everything needed fixing. Even the well would require a new pump.

This surely was not the farm of our dreams. This not the place where we might relax, enjoy life, and live economically. Manifest everywhere was the need for exhausting work, and a bank account as deep as the well. It was not for me.

And yet, looking across the level acres at the aquamarine mountains in the distance, and then up at the imposing mansion that stood proudly a ruin in the midst of ruin, I had the feeling that a property built with such integrity and such handsome dreams ought again to be fulfilled. Someone should restore what the original owner and builder had intended it to be forever: a symbol of staunch and honest living; symbol, too, of an age now gone when man was inspired to work hard so that he might enjoy the fruits of his labor. But I belonged to another era, and the aristocracy this estate symbolized was a tradition my generation had discarded. No, I was not the man to restore Gaston Hall.

Therefore I decided to get away quickly, and never return. That the place might grow on me, I already knew too well. The virus of ostentation is contagious, exciting both the ego and the imagination. Every man wants to be a king—and to live like one. But it is a destructive fever, destroying the sinew of intellectual progress and substituting a fatty tissue of self-contentment, the inevitable symptom of disintegration.

When I returned to the house, Lampert was howling and forgotten, although his lunchtime was long overdue, and Margaret stood in the hall facing the front door, her arms folded, one foot tapping the oil-stained floor. She made a few casual remarks which indicated that she had already selected bedrooms for her potential family of nine, had moved the kitchen from the basement to the butler's pantry off the dining room, had converted one wing into a gymnasium, the other into a library for me, and was fast draping the windows and telling the moving van people to put this piece right here and carry that one up to the first room on the right, head of the stairs.

Quickly I hurried her away, through the rear window. This time I drove, and I drove fast. I could not get away from there rapidly enough. Margaret seemed quite content to leave, but this did not surprise me. It was all too evident that she planned to return.

CHAPTER THREE

A DETERMINED woman has an answer to everything.

"See how pale Lampert is," Margaret said a few evenings later, although so far as I could see this fat butterball we called a son glowed with vitamin D sufficiency. "He needs to get out in the country where he can lie in the sun." That he had been in a playpen on the lawn for half the day was inconsequential. City sunlight is, to the woman bent on country living, like sunrays through glass: the healthful quality is filtered out of it.

We had not mentioned Gaston Hall since our Sunday drive. But Margaret had called attention to the layers of unhealthy dust in the apartment, which previously had always seemed to respond to a little dusting but now would not. She had built a personal tragedy out of the failure of a petunia bed to grow, blaming the anemic city soil; I did not mention that a watering can, judiciously used, would encourage her flowers. She began to complain of claustrophobia in our tiny cigar-box apartment, and I did not remind her that when we moved in, she had been delighted that a minimum of housekeeping would be required in this small space.

Like the retired naval officer in one of the towns of my

youth who, when harassed by his wife's complaining, ran
storm signals up on a flagpole in his back yard but said no
word, I kept a weather eye on the gathering hurricane of
discontent, yet did not comment. Sometimes, as when a
wife asks cautious questions about a blonde her husband
knew years before, it is wise to smile and say nothing. This
was such a time.

I did say, however, along about Thursday, that I had
been delegated as duty officer on Sunday, so she would not
get ideas for a Sabbath drive to see the flowering dogwood,
which was then in bloom in all the woods of Northern
Virginia and nowhere more radiantly, no doubt, than in
Orange County. So Sunday passed, the heralded auction sale
of Gaston Hall was set for Tuesday, and I was secure in
military duties that forbade any southward trip on the tenth
of May.

Just to make sure, though Margaret had never once dealt
me a card from the bottom of the deck, I took the car to the
Pentagon on Tuesday morning instead of the bus. Margaret
made no objection. In fact, she stood in the door as I departed, with Lampert in her arms, and waved his tiny hand
at me. This touching domestic scene insinuated in me a
reluctant indecision. We could not afford Gaston Hall.
The place would sell for more than we had on hand, even if
we dug into our modest nest egg, which we were determined
not to do. But at least, I thought, we might have been able
to contrive some way of driving down for the sale, just out
of curiosity as to its future ownership.

Thus I arrived at my military post softened up. The morning was blue and balmy, fully awakened to the exotics of
springtime, a perfect day for a drive in the country. The
memory of Margaret and Lampert, waving so cheerily from
the door, Margaret taking what must be acute disappoint-

ment without a word or a sign of complaint, touched me deeply. Surely she was as aware as I that this was the tenth of May. Most reluctantly, I approached my desk, wishing with all my heart that we could drive to Orange County—not of course to buy; merely to look.

This reverie was broken abruptly by a hurried summons to the office of General Norstad. I should have suspected foul play right then. General Norstad, unlike some of the star-shouldered military leaders, never peremptorily summoned anyone. Benign and gentle, he drove men beyond their resources by trust rather than arrogance. He inspired loyalty by kindness, made his staff feel that they were associates rather than hirelings, in every enterprise. Not even when General Arnold was walking the ceiling and throwing around his brass did Norstad yield to the heavy pressure upon him by hurling, in turn, a lead pipe at a helpless lieutenant colonel. So to be summoned to his office was cause for suspicion. Yet in war one becomes accustomed to reversals of character, and I entered his office alert but unsuspecting.

"You were duty officer Sunday," he said.

"Yes, sir."

"Today's mission (we were in the headquarters of the Twentieth Air Force, whose B-29 bombers were beginning to close in on Japan) has been postponed twenty-four hours. You'll be up all night tomorrow. It's a beautiful day. Go out and soak up some sunshine."

"But . . ."

"That's all."

When a general says "That's all" to a lieutenant colonel, he means it.

"Yes, sir," I said. General Norstad smiled.

When I reached home, Margaret was in street clothes,

and Lampert was in his best sweater suit, a present from my sister which he had never worn before.

"Oh!" she greeted me gaily. "We were just going out."

"I have the day off," I said. "Let's go down and see that sale at Gaston Hall. We can just about make it if we hurry."

Little manifestations become important only after the fact. What woman, faced suddenly with a change of plans, does not also change her dress? What mother of an infant, anticipating a long day away from home, does not spend a half hour in the kitchen, putting formulas in bottles, sterilizing nipples, packing a canvas bag against her child's lack of muscular control? We did not even return to the house. The canvas bag appeared, fully packed, from the baby buggy in which, of course, Lampert was to have been taken riding. We were in the car and on our way in thirty seconds.

We arrived a half hour before the sale. A large crowd appeared to be gathering, much to my satisfaction. The more bidders, the higher the price, the less likelihood that we would succumb to the temptation to buy this monumental ruin. We walked into the woods behind the house, into a forest I had not previously explored. Giant white oak and tulip poplar trees were everywhere.

"Whoever buys this place," I said, "could get some of his money back cutting this timber. There must be a good ten thousand dollars worth here."

"In that case," said the practical Margaret, "couldn't we afford to bid a little higher?"

We had agreed, on the way down, that if the place could be bought cheaply, we would buy; but we would not be stampeded by the excitement of an auction into paying more than a definite, coolly calculated sum.

"No," I said, "because the book says you should always add about twenty per cent to any estimate of remodeling to cover unforeseen expenses, and this timber would be something to fall back on."

"It's a capital gain," Margaret coaxed.

This being her first practical comment on money matters and taxes in all our married life (and her last, I might add) I was surprised, to say the least. Even then I did not suspect that she might have been coached, and that our walk in the woods was anything but accidental.

"It could be a beautiful place," I said as we returned to the front porch. "But don't set your heart on it. We haven't a chance."

Margaret's eyes grow very large on occasions of moment. She was not acting, now. She really wanted this reprobate establishment, this dissipated estate, this poverty-stricken symbol of outmoded living.

"I thought," I said, "that we were going to take life easy. What leisure would we have farming seven hundred acres, pouring money and our own labor down this rathole? Honestly, darling, I can't see it."

No tears, but almost.

"I tell you what I'll do," I said. "A few little improvements where they would show, and this place would sell for a lot more than we've agreed to pay for it. If I can get it at our price, I'll buy it. But remember that it's an investment, which also means carrying a big mortgage, and we'll turn it over."

Naturally, she agreed to that. She knew very well that if once she got her hands on it, it was hers for life.

"I can't bear to see you not get it," she said. "I'm not going to watch. I'll go sit in the car, and when you drop out, come on over."

So I faced the auctioneer alone, the responsibility and decision mine exclusively. A clever animal, is woman.

At the end of the sale, Margaret and I owned Gaston Hall. Margaret did not at first believe we had acquired the property. Someone went to her, introduced himself and said, "Congratulations. Your husband just bought Gaston Hall."

Slowly, without a word, Margaret climbed from the car.

"Now that it's yours," the man went on, "what on earth are you going to do with it?"

The question, coming from an outsider, brought Margaret up short. Day dreaming is one thing, ownership another. She was suddenly frightened, and for the first time unsure of herself. She looked up at the great house, woefully shabby from lack of paint, suspiciously unseaworthy of roof, and then out across the weed riot that once had been eighteen acres of lawn. She trembled a little and answered in a quavering voice.

"I really haven't the faintest idea," she said. At that moment, she meant it.

I was feeling very precocious about the whole business when I returned to the Pentagon next day. We had taken a long-shot gamble, and had won. In fairness I must say that I was as excited about it as was Margaret. The deadly virus already was at work. I was getting ideas by the minute. Most of all, I was the peacock preening his feathers. If I had not decided to go to the sale, luck should not have been ours. I was taking full credit, of that there was no doubt.

General Norstad put my feathers back where they belonged. Greeting me at staff meeting he said, "Well, did you buy the farm?"

I was stunned.

"Beg pardon, sir?" I fumbled, not sure I had heard aright.

"Did you buy the farm?" he repeated, and when I remained perplexed, he added, "Your wife was so eloquent on the phone, I didn't have the heart to turn her down."

"She called you?" I asked, heavily accenting both pronouns.

"Yes. Just before you left yesterday morning. She said your whole future was involved."

"Well," was all I could reply, "I guess there's no doubt about that."

CHAPTER FOUR

HEADY with the excitement of owner-
ship, Margaret and I waved aside the fact that our farm was
a complete catalogue of the hazards which the Department
of Agriculture had warned us against, including a staggering mortgage. In the comforting simplicity of our little
Washington apartment we began to make vast lists of the
miracles that we would perform at Gaston Hall. At least
we were aware that supernatural aid would be required.
Beyond that we were babes in our own woods.

Margaret summoned her mother from Nebraska to join
her for the gala ceremony of moving in. She did not warn
Stella, a practical woman, of the true state of affairs. Instead, her letter imploring her mother's company emphasized the seven hundred acres, the thirty-room house (including the eighteen basement cubicles), the eighteen acres
abloom to spring flowers, and the nine marble mantels.
Suspecting that perhaps Margaret's enthusiasm, perpetually
tinted with rosy colors, might in this instance have gone too
far, I leaned over Margaret's shoulder as she penned the
last paragraph of her letter. The exultant description of
Gaston Hall that assaulted me was more the reconstructed
than the actual condition of the premises.

"Better go a little easier," I said. "Your mother will come

with six dinner dresses to impress the butler, and what she needs for this job is a suitcase full of aprons."

Margaret ignored me. Already she saw her new home not as it was, but as it would one day be. Fortunately, her mother had been the victim of her enthusiasms before. She had been born on a Nebraska farm and knew what to expect from Margaret's casual comment, buried deep in the heart of her letter, that "the house has not been lived in for some time, although an old man has been existing here for many years." Hidden away in her luggage were a pair of sturdy shoes that could survive scrub water, a pair of rubber gloves, and several washable cotton work dresses. The remainder of her wardrobe was also practical, the handsome things a woman might slip into in a hurry if the neighbors began to call, and which in any event might be worn to church.

I did not know Stella well. A brief stay at her home in Lincoln, as a bridegroom on exhibition, was the extent of my acquaintance. She is tall, sturdy of character and physique, and sensible. Outwardly she suggests a slight timidity. This is misleading, for it stems not from shyness but from consideration for others, and from a natural caution that causes her to test a foundation before putting her whole weight on it. She will back away a mile from an awkward encounter, but when her mind is made up to face a situation she has it under control. She has an instinct for becoming part of any household without dominating it, an extremely agreeable trait in a mother-in-law, and is handy at what used to be called the feminine virtues: cooking, needlework, housekeeping, and stimulating conversation. She is also orderly, which trait I wish she had passed on to her daughter.

A woman of these accomplishments is handy to have around, especially when moving into an old house. I had

31

been anxious lest Margaret, turned loose with all her enthusiasms, would clutter up the place with broken antiques and other impractical furnishings. Somehow I thought that Stella would curb her daughter's optimisms. Even before Stella arrived I visualized mother and daughter at an auction sale, Margaret staggering the auctioneer with ferocious bids while her mother, a speculative frown upon her face, examined the proferred wares for decay and fraud. The stove of Margaret's gusto could not burn too hotly with such a damper. I also welcomed Stella because, when Margaret tackles anything, she does it with the wholehearted resolution of a puppy chewing on a shoe, impervious to the cries of unfed children or the laments of a neglected husband. Stella at least would feed Lampert at the proper hours if his mother was preoccupied with something else. And I also had the feeling that, if an intruder ventured into our lonely farmhouse, Stella would make him sorry he came. She is made of stern and agreeable stuff, my mother-in-law. I was lucky to get her.

She arrived in Washington the day before we were to drive down to Orange, the county seat of our new home, to pass the deed. The owner of the premises had returned from Florida for the sale. Since he had no place else to live, he had moved all his own goods into one wing of the house until he could advertise and sell them at auction, and had left a stallion in the pasture. Our furniture had been ordered shipped from a warehouse in New York and was expected to arrive simultaneously with us. Therefore the plan was for Margaret and her mother, with the baby, to stay on at the farm while I returned to my military duties.

Stella was impressed, as is everyone, with the first view of the big house. This time the front door stood open, so we did not use the back window, as formerly. Lampert's crib, a two-day reserve of baby food, and an automobile load of furnishings without which Margaret could not live even for a day, were unloaded to the front porch. Then I sped to town rapidly. I did not want to see Stella's face when she crossed that threshold for the first time.

I expected to return in an hour, but the deed did not pass quietly. The word had gone round that the old man was selling out, and a few relatives from whom he had borrowed money from time to time were on hand to collect. Each of them pressed his claim on me. There was the further complication that, while the deed rested in the name of a divorced wife, and her lawyer was on hand to sign her name, the old man's consent also was required and he, seeing a possible chance to balance the books with his creditors, placed a money value on his signature. Then there was the bank representative, protecting his mortgage equity, and several persons who, so far as I could determine, were mere spectators, though not silent ones. The afternoon dragged on in a series of piques and wrangles.

Finally, at ten minutes to five, with the courthouse in which the deed must be registered ready to close for the night, a happy inspiration hit me.

"I don't know anything about your business, or your side deals, or what's going on here," I said. "But if this deed is not signed in two minutes, I will just send my check to the divorced wife and you can all whistle to her. Let her decide how much money you all get, not I."

This had a remarkable effect. The old man gave his consent, the lawyer signed, the tax stamps were affixed. I threw my check on the table and raced to the courthouse. The clerk was locking up, but was obliging. He had just handed me my receipt when the entire gang I had just left rushed in, shouting to the clerk to hold up his work. My check, it

33

seemed, was not certified, and it was on a Connecticut bank although I resided in Washington, a suspicious circumstance to say the least.

This matter was important to all concerned for meanwhile they had agreed how the money was to be divided, and the banker, after taking out his mortgage, was to make disbursements to the whole tribe. He did not fear for his mortgage, because the real estate could not walk away, but he did have visions of paying out substantial cash amounts to a half dozen persons, none of whom lived in the vicinity.

Another ten minutes of artful haggling ensued, while the county clerk, his eye on the clock, proceeded to lock his vaults and don his hat and coat. My lawyer, who all afternoon had worn the look of a Virginia gentleman who could not believe that people really talked like those now before him, finally penetrated the impasse.

"I hardly think," he said with great dignity and extreme casualness, "that Mr. Spence would introduce himself to our community with a bad check. It is my understanding he intends to live here."

The banker took the hint, accepted his responsibility, and walked out the door, the whole swarm after him. The clerk pointedly said, "Good night."

"And the deed?" I asked.

"Passed," the clerk said laconically, "inscribed and entered in the deed book. I hope you enjoy Gaston Hall more than its previous owner—and have better luck there." He glanced significantly at my lawyer and held open the door.

When I reached the farm I saw the stallion grazing the front lawn. Margaret was still scrubbing, on hands and knees, in the same room as when I left. Stella was nowhere in sight.

34

"This place," Margaret said tensely, her gaiety gone, "is just a plain mess."

I was in no position to give help or comfort, since my train to Washington was due. I found Stella in the basement, just abandoning an attempt to clear a chimney flue of twenty years accumulation of soot so she could start an old wood-burning stove. Her hair straggled about her eyes; her hands were black to above the wrist. She smiled, however, as though she had never been happier.

"You'd better go to the hotel tonight," I suggested.

"Looking like this?" Stella asked. "We'll make out all right."

Stella's many gifts do not, apparently, include prescience, for what happened that night should have caused us to quit the farm, take our loss philosophically, and reconcile ourselves to urban living on a modest scale. Having returned to Washington, I took no part in what followed, but I heard all about it by mail a few days later. By seven o'clock Margaret had one room cleaned, though the furniture for it had not arrived. The electricity in the house worked, but there was no way to cook anything. Water pressure, under the demands of scrubbing, had diminished little by little and finally, about sundown, trickled out altogether. So there were Margaret and Stella at dusk, with no heat to warm the baby's formula, no water either for bath or supper, no stove for cooking, and no beds on which to sleep.

A quick reconnaissance turned up the key to the wing in which the former owner's goods were stored. Evidently he had not used a mattress, or had removed it from the premises. A large sofa was found, however, with a spring seat which might serve as a bed. The women found it too heavy to lift, so they took the seat from it to the library and made up a litter on the floor. Fortunately, ample bedding and

35

Lampert's crib had been brought from Washington. Margaret drove to the crossroads store, heated Lampert's milk, and brought home some crackers and cheese.

About this time Margaret's mother began to doubt the success of the enterprise.

"We are just two women alone on this great big farm," she said. "I think we'd be safer upstairs tonight."

So the sofa seat was lugged aloft, the baby crib after it. This necessitated sweeping more filth from a bedroom. The place could not be scrubbed; there was no water. By ten o'clock the inhabitants of Gaston Hall were too weary for further labor. Hungry, dirty, they lay down to sleep.

Then the rats, rightful tenants by years of squatter possession, began to reassert their claim. Up and down the staircase, across the floors they ran, until Stella arose, went to the car, and returned with the tire jack which she put on the floor convenient to her hand.

Now unaccustomed farm noises chorused about the house. Silences are relative, particularly in the country. The clamor of katydids in the trees covered ominous undertones. The tumultuous courtship of the tree toads masked furtive footfalls. Through the din of nocturnal nature the two women concentrated their hearing to separate and identify the alien sounds.

Soon an intermittent swishing welled up out of the silences into a significant signal. The first thought was of a snake. The sound was close at hand, possibly in the English ivy outside the window. Stella, the hardier spirit, at last arose to investigate. The hiss was the gentle scrape of a hickory limb against the screen.

Laughing with relief, Margaret and her mother resolved to sleep. The rats began to scamper again. By deep and steady breathing Margaret simulated slumber, as did Stella, neither deceiving the other. Margaret recalled a story she had read somewhere, in which a rat had bitten off a baby's nose. She went to Lampert, found him safe and somnolent. Returning to her mattress, Margaret finally slept.

She awoke to find Stella's hand tightly clutching her arm. In rigid silence she lay a moment, pitching her ear under the caterwaul of the katydids and tree toads for the noise that had alarmed her mother. She heard the tinkle of breaking class.

"Someone is breaking a window on the first floor," Stella whispered. The sound was bolder now.

Stella leaped up, car jack in hand. She might be terrified of snakes and rats, but never of mortal man.

"Mother, don't!" Margaret whispered. Stella continued on her way, Margaret dallying only long enough to assure herself again that Lampert was undisturbed. They crept down the darkened stairs, their bare feet gummy from the grimy accumulation of years. They felt their way around unaccustomed corners toward the back door, where the disturbance centered. Stella raised the jack over her head, and lunged across a path of moonlight to the door. A startled face met hers. Stella laughed.

The visage was that of the old stallion, sad and hungry outside the door. Sensible animal that he was, he foraged for food in the garbage pail, at the same time tramping with his feet a pile of broken crockery and glass that Margaret and her mother had shoveled from the house.

To the stallion, this may not have been amusing, but hysterical relief caught up with the women. The stallion must have thought them silly indeed. One, her hair in curlers, clutching an auto jack; the other, in a frail nightie which the moon alone could appreciate and reach out to touch, they sat on the porch steps and laughed until the stallion moved away.

As they returned upstairs, they observed the dim outline of the steps. Dawn had come. They slept.

By the time I arrived to spend the day on the following Sunday, Margaret was again in high spirits, although I did not detect much enthusiasm in Stella. The plumbing was in repair, the cylinder oil was gone from the floors, an electric stove operated in the butler's pantry, and Margaret had discovered how to get things done. Over this last she was jubilant.

I should mention that our daughter Laurie, at that time unborn, was becoming conspicuous. The Virginian, a gentleman even in this decadent day, refuses any woman little, and a pregnant one nothing. Margaret, frustrated by artisans who would make few promises and keep none, discovered that if she made of her supplications a personal appearance, all remonstrance and delay ended. Workmen, tradesmen, handymen all hurried to do her bidding as soon as they saw her. And she, base soul, capitalized on their gallantry. By resourcefulness and an obviously fruitful body, she had done wonders with the house in five days.

I thought I detected in Margaret's manner a slight belligerence, however. She had saved several chores for me to do, all involving the use of a scrub brush. Each time I took my bucket to the faucet she would drop her own work and inquire, "Is there enough water?"

The time came, along toward noon, when my answer was negative. Far from disturbed, Margaret beamed.

"All right," she said, "I'll show you about it."

The government bulletin, in regard to water, says the supply should be constant and free flowing. Ours was constant, all right, accumulated over a watershed of two hundred acres of ungrazed woodland and collected in a well

38

more than one thousand feet deep. The free flowing part was something else again.

The house supply system extended from this deep well to a standpipe in the back park, from which it circulated by gravity to a dozen outlets, including the main residence. So gentle was the grade behind the house that the third floor was about even with the top of the standpipe. Consequently, to keep water in the third floor bathroom required an over-flowing reservoir. As the water in storage diminished, the second floor water outlets next suffered from lack of pressure, then the first floor, and finally the basement. There was always time, when the kitchen faucets gasped and went dry, to hurry to the basement and salvage enough water to boil a pot of tea.

Margaret had battled the water situation all week long. When the reservoir was empty, she went to the pump house, about one hundred yards away at the foot of a hill, cranked an insolent gasoline engine, then ran up the hill to open a valve at the base of the standpipe. After about four hours the standpipe overflowed, and water coursing down its brick sides signaled Margaret to turn off the engine, and race back up the hill to close the valve before all the water just pumped ran back into the well. Experts, including the government pamphlet No. 1460, *Simple Plumbing Repairs,* state that a check valve may be installed to open and close under pressure, thus eliminating the one hundred yard dash. The thing doesn't work, though; I installed one.

Margaret explained to me in some detail the vicissitudes of obtaining water, and her voice took on a distinct tone of martyrdom as she hinted how to start the engine. The trick there, as nearly as I could interpret her lay description of combustion principles, was that the pump started without gasoline, then required voracious quantities to keep it firing.

39

The gas line must not be opened until the machine had begun to work. The thing also kicked, she warned me, not in the predictable manner of the Model T Ford, but with a capricious devilishness, as though it was determined to break one's arm every time—in two places. That this engine squatted solidly on a concrete floor complicated the matter, too, for one had to get down on his knees to reach the crank handle. Margaret defied me to learn, as had she, to jump backward while on my knees. The floor where this kneeling took place, incidentally, was puddled with grease and oil.

Margaret did not accompany me to the well house. Even when fifteen minutes elapsed, without the awful clatter that attended the engine when it took hold, she remained on the porch step. I was about to give up when, without warning of any kind, the machine turned over and the pump began to revolve. I had taken off the belt between pump and engine to make it crank more easily, and now I could not replace the belt. After a moment's warm-up, I shut off the engine, sure that it would start again. I replaced the belt, which was sticky with alemite, and gave the engine a confident flip. Nothing happened. Another flip. Another. A long spin. Nothing. I was right back where I had started. Again I removed the belt, wiped the grime from my hands, knelt on the oily floor, and cranked. The next I knew I was lying in the doorway, the engine banging resolutely before me. Evidently I had been kicked so hard that my head had banged against the wall, knocking me out. This time I managed to secure the belt and raced up the hill, bringing the gate valve under control.

When I returned to the porch, oil-soaked, begrimed, and bruised, Margaret was not even sympathetic.

"That's what I've been doing all week," she said, and went back to her work.

40

Just then, down the hill in the pump house, the engine noise died away. I had forgotten to open the gas line.

My next encounter was with a refrigerator. This does not sound particularly menacing, but little complications have a way of becoming monumental complexities in the country, far from skilled repairmen.

Margaret had searched the countryside and I the Washington shops for a fortnight in quest of an electric refrigerator. In anticipation of the teeming provender we planned to raise on the farm, we had in mind a box of at least thirty cubic feet, and none of any size was procurable. Summer meanwhile was coming on, while Lampert's formula soured on a table. Margaret had tried putting milk, eggs, and meat in the well house, but it kept disappearing. Even a lock on the door did not stop the theft, nor were there any evidences of footprints in the soft dirt outside.

At this time, though still stationed in Washington, I was able to visit the farm almost every Saturday. One morning, in midweek, I received an urgent letter from Margaret, about as follows:

"We simply must get a refrigerator somewhere. This morning I took Lampert with me and we went down to the well house to get some eggs for lunch. The lock on the door had not been touched, so quite confidently I unlocked it and carried Lampert inside. You know it's gloomy in there and I couldn't see very well, but I knew about where everything was. I was feeling around for the eggs when suddenly a large skunk trundled past me and went out the door. Fortunately for both Lampert and me, he did not fire his artillery as he went by. The eggs were all gone and the butter ruined. If you want to eat when you come down Saturday (I hope you make it as planned) you had better bring a refrigerator with you."

I advertised my need in the Washington *Star*. Next day a man telephoned that he had just the thing. It was a forty-cubic-foot wooden box, lead-lined and, he admitted, rather old. It worked from a compressor that could be rigged up in the basement with ease. He knew it would work in the country, since it had been on his own farm, and he'd let me have it, with all the copper tubing, fittings, and necessities for three hundred dollars.

I bought it sight unseen.

Then the man said, "You'd better bring a good big truck, and some heavy jacks, because this thing is on the floor of my barn and it weighs fourteen hundred pounds."

Early Saturday morning I hired a truck, sent Margaret a telegram to have eight husky men on hand at the farm about noon, and went out to get my purchase. It looked fine. It was big, all right, with twelve double-glass doors. In fact, it reminded me of something out of a delicatessen. The compressor was formidable in appearance, but should be no mystery to the neighborhood auto mechanic. I trucked it the hundred miles to the farm, feeling very smug about the whole business. Margaret, I knew, would love me for this.

She had recruited eight field hands from neighboring farms and awaited me. There was only one way to move the contraption—right through the front doors. With much grunting, heaving, and a dexterous fitting of wooden rollers, we shoved the box over groaning floors into the butler's pantry, which Margaret was making over into a kitchen. A huge iron safe that had been in the pantry had been removed, necessitating the removal also of the door frame. The refrigerator fitted perfectly the hole in the side wall with an inch to spare. Margaret was jubilant. She tipped her muscled helpers liberally and telephoned the auto mechanic, an obliging, agreeable fellow named Colvin who, I discovered on his arrival, was now almost a fixture on our premises, since he had the gift for starting the water pump.

Mr. Colvin eyed the box approvingly, and allowed that it ought to work without much trouble. He went to the basement to see how to route the copper tubing through the floor while Margaret, after giving me a hearty kiss, assembled all her perishables and put them in the new refrigerator.

A moment later Mr. Colvin returned to the kitchen, his face an apology.

"Mrs. Spence," he said hesitantly, as befitted the occasion, "I'm most terribly afraid this box isn't going to do."

The rejoicing in the kitchen was cut as by the appearance of a creditor.

"Why not?" I said. "The man I bought it from guaranteed it would work."

"It'll work, all right," Mr. Colvin said. "There's no doubt about that. But it won't work here."

"Why?" I had not laid out three hundred dollars, truck rental, and tips for eight hands for nothing. This refrigerator was going to work, or else.

"The compressor down there is water cooled," Mr. Colvin said, his voice as solemn as judgment day. He hated to articulate what he must say, and every syllable parted from him with great reluctance. "With that pump you got you'll never get enough water to keep this compressor cool—and if you try to keep the pump going constantly, it'll never stand the strain. I welded it in two places yesterday, and it's about gone."

So there we were. The plumber in town confirmed Mr. Colvin's findings. He suggested that the solution was to put in an electric pump for another four hundred dollars

—if, war shortages considered, he could find a pump and enough pipe to go a thousand feet down our well. Even then, he admitted, our electric bill to run the compressor would probably be twenty-five dollars a month, and it would mean running 220-volt current into the house. If we did that, we'd have to put in a new electric outlet box, as the one we had would never pass a fire insurance underwriter in its present state; the switch was cracked. Cost? Oh, conservatively the job might be done for two hundred fifty dollars—if he could find an outlet box; they were pretty scarce.

So we put the forty-cubic-foot refrigerator on the back porch and advertised for a buyer. None came along at any price. Margaret sold the compressor separately for fifty dollars and with it bought an old-fashioned icebox to tide her over.

Meanwhile the refrigerator with its twelve doors stood, an unsightly reminder of my folly, on the back porch for more than a year. One day Lampert was lost. Margaret hunted all over the farm for him, underneath the porches, in the swimming pool (which was clogged with six feet of muddy water) and in a stream that runs below the house. Finally, almost in collapse, she sat down on the back porch to consider where Lampert might be. She heard a faint rapping that seemed to come from the old refrigerator. Looking up she saw her baby through the double glass. He had crawled into the box and closed the door after him.

That day the three-hundred-dollar investment in refrigeration was moved from the porch into the deep woods, the doors taken off their hinges and buried separately. Agriculture Leaflet No. 1868, *Protecting Your Wild Life*, says that an old refrigerator makes an ideal hutch for wild rabbits. So far as I am concerned, they are welcome to it.

CHAPTER FIVE

T HE next urgent necessity was to secure a farmer. Stella was anxious to return home, her spouse being of the opinion, to which he gave stronger articulation daily by letter and telephone, that what had begun as a little visit was rapidly becoming a case of desertion.

Stella refused to leave, however, as long as her departure would leave Margaret completely alone on the farm, except for Lampert who, at fourteen months, could scarcely classify as a protector even under war manpower conditions.

On the subject of agricultural labor, Margaret and I were well fortified by expert advice. Government pamphlet DS21, *Getting Established on the Land*, told us all we needed to know except where to find a farmer. We were determined that whoever we hired must be indigenous to the local environment. A stranger would not know where to find day labor, or from whom to borrow a disc harrow, or who had that most useful of all farm implements, the cement mixer; or, of course, to whom not to lend the new tractor. Also, he must be familiar with the peculiarities of the growing season in these parts, and possess a sensitivity to nature's vagaries that would help him to forecast the weather. Since we ourselves were strangers in the community, we hoped that whoever we hired on the farm would also know which of the local merchants were most reliable, and which skilled craftsmen really skillful.

Beyond these practical considerations, we also required a man who would be able to work with, and take orders from a woman. The Twentieth Air Force was at that time throwing out its wings into India, China, and soon to the islands of the Pacific, and with each new establishment my name came up as a possible member of the complement. Even if I remained in Washington for the duration, the accelerating tempo of air operations demanded more and more of everyone, and in the Pentagon I was now too busy to visit the farm frequently or for more than a few hours at a time.

Therefore, while I might on paper lay out an extensive program of repair and soil replenishment, as recommended by my collateral reading, Margaret would supervise it. Farmers are, in many cases, peculiar fellows who believe woman's place is in the kitchen and nursery, not in the tilled field.

As soon as we moved in, the ne'er-do-wells of the community pounced on us, seeking a new patron for their indolences. Farm help was so scarce that Margaret was tempted to hire the first man who appeared, a beady-eyed little fellow with a tobacco-stained mouth, who rolled up to the front door one morning in a Model A Ford which bulged with children. His description of his own qualifications was so extraordinary that Margaret became suspicious. Some instinct warned her to check with his previous employer. The recommendation she received was this: "Mrs. Spence, that shiftless no-account is the laziest man in these parts. He won't work, he's filthy dirty, and he's drunk all the time. His wife set his last house afire putting coal oil in the cook stove. I'm sure the county would be glad if you hired him —he's been on relief for three years. That's about all I can say about him except that he steals."

Fortunately, we did not have a telephone, for such a frank delineation of shortcomings would never have been elaborated except face to face. Margaret discovered this rural phenomenon when she checked on her next candidate, who had been so inarticulate that she was unable to extract much information from him. She went to the corner store and telephoned his current employer, a dairyman. She explained her errand.

"Yes," the dairyman said tentatively.

"Can you recommend him?"

"He's working for me."

"Is he good?"

"Well—he's a dairy hand. He has no responsibilities."

"Does that imply he is not capable of responsibility?"

"Oh, no."

After a few more inconclusive rejoinders, Margaret thanked him and ended the call. The storekeeper, who had listened attentively to all this, stepped forward.

"Mrs. Spence," she said cautiously, "why don't you go and *see* him?"

Something in the tone compelled Margaret to do so. The dairyman greeted her with a smile.

"Lord help you, child," he told Margaret, "I was about to get in my car and come over to your place. You don't want that fellow. I've given him thirty days to clear out, and I'd be delighted to have almost anyone hire him, just to get rid of him. But not a woman alone on a farm—that wouldn't do."

Margaret thanked him and turned to leave. "Why didn't you tell me that on the phone?" she asked.

The dairyman was positively astounded.

"On a fourteen-party line?" he asked.

The next several applicants were little better. One had

a hernia and could do no lifting. Another wanted his entire family, consisting of a wife and four children, boarded in our kitchen, since his wife had "athreetus" so bad she couldn't lay up a finger to help out. Another wanted two hundred dollars a month plus sustenance, and on no account would he milk on Saturday night or Sunday.

The book said not to be discouraged over the labor market, but to keep hunting until the right person came along. It was more economical, the Department of Agriculture warned, not to farm at all than to have the wrong help. Margaret continued her search, with advertisements in the county weekly paper.

One day I received, in Washington, a letter from the tidewater section of southern Virginia, signed Glee Willom. It said this man was a native of our county, had worked for eighteen years on a farm almost within sight of ours, and had been lured away a year previously by the high wages prevailing in the cotton country. He wanted to get home, he said, and I would find him a good hand, familiar with all types of machinery. He also added a postcript which said, "I can laid off a field for plowing without help."

Since this last was something I could not do, I was impressed. I was further interested because he had suggested I check his character with his former employer, a woman. If he had taken orders from a woman for eighteen years, he was just what we needed. Margaret's local investigation uncovered a unanimous community sentiment that we would be lucky to get him. An interview was arranged.

My prospect was a short, chunky man with a forearm like a piano leg and thighs the thickness of telephone poles. His whole body typified power, from his red, close-cropped hair, and a neck that would have been contemptuous of a size twenty-two collar, through his hogshead-stout chest and matching hips, below which, like foundations in the ground, stretched those remarkable legs. His face, blue-eyed and direct, was sober and cautious, as befitted a man who worked with nature, and there was a humorous crink at the corners of his mouth. He had brought his wife along, a little woman named Hazel with a pretty, high-cheekboned face, and I gathered from the anxious looks he cast occasionally at her that the decision was hers as much as his. She reminded me somewhat of a literary agent, waiting patiently through the negotiations until the talk turned to money, at which point she would take over. She wanted to see the house in which she would live. Oddly, however, she expressed no comment whatever once she had laid eyes on it, and did not even go inside.

Glee proved a cautious bargainer. Every sinew of his muscled torso professed what his face tried to hide, that he was anxious to sign on. He talked about farming methods in the cotton country, the bad climate there, the poor schools for his eight children. During all this he cast his eyes over as much of the farm as he could see, sizing up the job ahead of him.

I in turn discussed the farm and what I proposed to do to it. He looked dubious when, from my newly acquired book learning, I talked about sowing alfalfa without two years' preparation of the soil. He was positively depressed when I suggested "we" might cut enough timber to erect stout plank fences over our seven hundred acres. He was skeptical of the power equipment I proposed to buy, with its newfangled attachments such as a posthole digger, a scoop shovel, and a double-bottom plow that could be adjusted to cut the soil without turning it entirely over. Such notions were out of

49

the range of his experience, but he implied, by the concentration with which he attended my words, that he was willing to try.

"What are you going to stock?" he asked, finally.

"Until the farm is cleaned up and some pastures built, I'm just getting a couple of carloads of steers. They'll help to clear out the trash, and then we'll go on from there."

"No dairy?"

"No. Just a couple of milk cows for the farm."

"My husband ain't working in no dairy," his wife, Hazel, put in.

Glee took this entirely in stride, as though he was accustomed to it.

"Milkin' isn't my line," he said.

"We don't have the right buildings for a dairy," I said.

"Nice level fields you got," Glee said. "When I was a boy I used to think how easy this land would plow."

"Glee nearly kilt a man once," his wife injected abruptly. "He got called a dirty name in a store, and he butted this fellow with his head so hard they busted right out through the screen door. They had to set a fire under 'em to get 'em apart. My Glee don't take no talk off nobody."

"I'm sure he doesn't," I said.

Glee hitched up his pants. "Well?" he said.

We settled the details then, and much to my surprise, Hazel did not negotiate. She listened but said not a word, although several times I felt she was a prompter in the wings, anxious lest her actor in this drama forget his lines. In such crises her shoulders twitched impatiently, she leaned forward and concentrated on transferring her urgent thoughts to Glee. Shyly he looked over at her, caught his cue, and resumed his bargaining. Hazel relaxed then until she decided he had forgotten something else, when the performance

50

was repeated, with the same result. The psychic accord between the two was phenomenal.

They were not much concerned with the wages. The discussion surrounded the "findings" Glee would receive in addition to his cash pay. He insisted on receiving one hundred pounds of white flour a month, about twice the county standard. I did not appreciate that a family of ten needed such a quantity of flour, but Glee was adamant. I cut his quota of corn meal proportionately. He also required four hundred pounds of meat. This is little more than a pound a day, and I agreed, although it was high for the neighborhood. I provided a gallon of milk daily, if we had it on the farm, a house equipped with a heating stove, all the wood Glee needed for both cooking and heating stoves, and an acre of garden space. I declined to allow him to work his vegetables on my time, which he appeared to think unreasonable. To offset this rebuff, he sought to procure an unlimited quantity of barley and corn from my granary to feed two hogs he proposed to keep in a pen near his house. This I rejected most emphatically and, since he did not insist on the point, I crowded my advantage and put an embargo on chickens, also. I limited him to one dog.

"Now," I said, "the important thing—when can you start?"

He grinned boyishly and turned to his wife.

"We already quit at Smithfield," she informed me. "My baby got swamp fever down there and I just said, 'Glee, there's a time to stay and a time to quit, and this is the time to go.'"

"I didn't know you had a baby," I said. "How old?"

"Nine years," Hazel answered.

The family moved in next day; Glee cut himself some firewood and went to work. I was not there on his arrival, having returned to Washington, but I left him a formidable list of things to do. A few days later the entire county knew what we proposed to do with Gaston Hall. Margaret asked Glee about this and he admitted, though reluctantly, "The Colonel's list is pretty complicated. I got the storekeeper to read it to me, to be sure I understood it right."

Margaret's concern was for a large vegetable garden, and she asked Glee to attend to that detail first. He made ready the land and then for two sunny days planted nothing. He did go out and buy us a dairy cow, bargaining shrewdly, and hired a day hand named Benny to do the milking. This accomplished, he and his new assistant set to work with a grubbing hoe hacking away patches of weeds.

Margaret watched this from the kitchen window for a day and a half, before she inquired what had happened to the vegetable planting.

"The sign's in the foot," Glee said. "Most people say it's good for killing weeds, or weaning calves, but no good for planting. Tomorrow's a good day. We'll get in the root crops and greens and then Thursday the potatoes."

"You mean," Margaret said, "that one day is better than another to plant a row of carrots?"

Glee looked at Benny in abject shame that he had hired himself to such an ignoramus.

"Most people around here goes by the almanac," Glee explained patiently. "It's best that way. You'll discover."

Glee had a day for everything. He waited eight days to set several hens because his almanac listed only one occasion during the month for that activity. If Margaret proposed to plant a seed bed, Glee assented readily, but kept himself busy, with one excuse or another until the best day was at hand.

He knew the lore of the countryside and its import. One

afternoon Margaret mentioned, over the milk bucket, that she planned to wash clothes the next morning.

"The branch (that's a creek in these parts) is rising this evening, ma'am," Glee said. "Rain tomorrow." He was right, too.

There was some confusion over terminology. "Evening" to Glee was the daylight between noon dinner and evening supper. During a dry spell, worried that the boxwood required water and not wanting to burn the plants by wetting them in the heat of the day, Margaret asked Glee if, as a special favor, he would do that work "this evening." He did it, immediately after lunch.

I had ordered two carloads of Texas steers. By the time they arrived Glee had fenced a field to contain them. With the new tractor he spent two diligent days mowing the pastures. When next I visited the farm, the evidences of tenancy were impressive, including new sheeting on a barn roof from which the tin had been blown by a storm prior to our ownership.

Glee had made himself handy to Margaret, too. He emptied trash barrels without being asked, piled on the porch a stack of wood for the fireplaces and, morning and night, inquired whether she needed anything done. Margaret noticed that if, in the middle of the night, Lampert required attention and she turned on a light, Glee soon appeared on the walk beneath her window. Plainly, he had worked for a woman before.

When I talked to him, he had only one complaint and was reluctant even to discuss it. Finally, after some coaxing, he hitched up his pants with a gesture I was soon to recognize as one of acute embarrassment, and spoke.

"Colonel . . ." he said tentatively.

"Yes, Glee?"

53

"Mind, I'm not complaining."

"I understand, Glee."

"I want to do right by you in every way."

"That works both ways," I said.

He scratched his ear with a pudgy finger, sighed, and plunged, but he smiled, in true Virginia fashion, when he

said it. "Your wife has a sofa about eight feet long, and it's all in one piece. Colored green."

"Yes?"

"Me and Benny hefted that thing up into a bedroom the other day. Nigh ruptured me."

"I'm sorry, Glee."

"Oh, that's all right, only—" he paused again, "next day we toted it down again."

"I'm terribly sorry," I said.

"Yesterday we lugged it upstairs again—to a different room."

"I'll speak to Mrs. Spence about it," I said.

"I'd appreciate it," he said, and with the deep sigh of a reluctant witness who has confessed all and is happy for it, he walked away.

CHAPTER SIX

THE appearance of Glee made us feel that at last we had begun to plant our roots. True, the growth was shallow, like that of the boxwood, but durable, and despite Margaret's feverish efforts to make her house livable and to supervise the expanding complications of farm work, the security of permanence gave her peace of mind. I, in Washington, at last had a place to call home.

Only one neighbor called that first summer. Margaret had settled on the farm during corn planting time in early May, preamble to a strenuous harvest season. The young people were all at war, so the older folks were inundated by the jobs their juniors had formerly done. There were three murders within a mile of us, too, and I think the local inhabitants were shy to call on Margaret, lest they be drawn into a discussion of these shames. Inasmuch as the felonies all involved carnal knowledge, as it is called hereabouts, Margaret did not even hear of them; for Glee, the soul of discretion, did not consider crimes of passion fit subjects for discourse with his lady employer.

A few days after Stella left for home, Margaret had a brief flurry of contact with "the county." First, a car she recognized as that of a prominent neighbor swept up the drive at nine o'clock one morning. Spying it at a distance, Margaret quickly threw the clutter of children's toys into a stairway, dumped her unscrubbed son onto the back porch, raced upstairs for a fresh apron, and managed to reach the door shortly after its second ring.

"Come in," she invited cheerily.

"No," was the chilly answer. "This is not a social call. I just want to borrow your manure spreader."

That same week, also early in the morning, a station wagon with the name of a large farm emblazoned on it stopped at the front door. This time, remembering her earlier rebuff, Margaret answered the bell without even setting down the dustmop. This was a mistake. Her visitor was definitely calling, and quite formally, to make Margaret's acquaintance and to invite her and me to Sunday lunch the next time I was at the farm.

With these exceptions, the county left Margaret alone. In consequence, Margaret's orientation to community folkways was limited to her contacts with the farm hands. This gave her opportunity to master the colloquial speech. Glee's son Obed, for example, who worked both on the farm and in the house, had a southern accent so thick that for months Margaret did not understand it. To her, the nuances of Virginia articulation and the subtleties of the Virginia mind were equally confusing.

She learned one characteristic of the county in a hurry, however. No one ever gave her a definite answer to anything. No one ever said "no." Conversely, no one ever said "yes," either. The Virginia working man will not commit himself on any subject. If he promised to do a day's work and then, on that date, decided to go fishing, he would be in the position of breaking his word, which no Virginian on any social level will do. I suspect also, that no Virginian will work if the almanac is right for fishing.

Particularly, Margaret wanted to get some painting and brick masonry done about the house. She sent Glee out, in the car, to run down the proper artisan. He returned from these searches and reported.

Margaret said, "Well, did you find someone?"

"Yes, ma'am. Harold Carpenter, he'll be along."

"Oh, that's fine, Glee. Thanks very much. When is Mr. Carpenter coming?"

"I couldn't directly say."

"Will he be here tomorrow?"

"Well, he might."

"Did he say he would?"

"No, ma'am, but I reckon he might. Again he might not."

"Why?"

"Well, I dunno. But don't you worry, he'll come."

Mr. Carpenter showed up two weeks later, on a morning Margaret was away attending an auction sale.

When a water pipe burst in the kitchen, Margaret turned off the main valve to the standpipe and telephoned, from the crossroads store, to the town plumber. She explained the nature of her emergency.

"I'll try to help you out," the plumber said.

"Today?" Margaret pinned him down.

"Well, I'll see what I can do for you."

"But I must know," Margaret insisted. "If you can't manage to come today, I'll have to find someone else."

"Don't worry, lady," the plumber reassured her. "I'll work you in as soon as I can, but I can't tell just when it will be."

His crew was on the job within an hour.

When workmen appeared, they gave themselves wide latitude for the completion of their tasks. Two jacklegs employed to make urgent repairs to Glee's roof finally came

58

to work a month after they had been engaged. In two days, they had almost finished and Margaret wanted to be sure that they returned on the morrow. At quitting time she went to them.

"You don't have much left to do," she said.

"No, ma'am," the boss said. "One more morning will finish it."

"I don't want to leave all that roof uncovered if it rains," Margaret said. "You will come back tomorrow and put on the shingles, won't you?"

The workman thought about that a moment.

"I'll try," he said.

"But it's got to be done," Margaret replied emphatically. "Rain would ruin the house, and tomorrow's Friday, and I know you won't work Saturday, and it's bound to rain over the week end. Please come tomorrow."

"If nothing turns up," the carpenter said.

A week later Glee and Benny climbed to the roof, during a rain, and put on the last shingles.

Margaret analyzed this caution, in a letter to me, and came up with an answer to it. The handymen in these parts are a proud lot. They will not admit their limitations. If a carpenter, for example, tears out part of a chimney while repairing a roof, he will not ask that a brick mason be summoned. He will take the job as far as he can go, then walk off and never return. One of my neighbors contracted for a new barn, and the workmen made, for this countryside, remarkable time on the job. In only eight months they had the building up, except for two metal ventilators on the roof. All one day they fussed about, trying to figure out how to set the ventilators. Then they disappeared. Two years passed before the ventilators finally were put in place—by someone else.

Farm employees are the same way, with a slight variation. There are jobs they do not like to do, consequently they avoid them. Glee would scheme for a week over a subterfuge rather than milk our three dairy cows even once. He would construct elaborate arguments for the retention on the farm of a useless hand, if the man is a good milker. Likewise, Glee would not clean out a drainage ditch. For two years I scheduled some ditching work for Glee to do. It was not intricate and could have been accomplished in half a day. Glee never got around to it. His ingenuity in manufacturing excuses was formidable. I dare say I asked him forty times why that ditching had not been done. Each time he gave me a new, and irrefutable, alibi. In the end, I had to call in a steam shovel operator.

Our day hand, Benny, was a font of colloquial information for Margaret that first summer. Benny is a genial, happy-go-lucky Negro who owns a two-story house and four acres in the woods, and thus is independent. He is perhaps sixty-five now, though some say he has passed his seventieth year. His is an ageless frame, tall, big-boned, and powerful. No one has ever accused him of idling at his work. Getting him on the job is something else. Long years ago, Benny figured out how much money a week he needs to insure his living. He earns that much and no more. When we first came in contact with him, he put in four days a week, though we never knew what four days they would be. Now, with higher wages, his requirements necessitate only two and one-half days of work a week. These Benny gives us; not an hour more.

Benny had been employed, at one time or another, by everyone in the vicinity. He doesn't like to stay put. He keeps moving on. Give him a suit of clothes, or lend him a few dollars, and he promptly goes to work for someone else.

I challenged him on this point one time, when he sought to borrow five dollars to pay his taxes.

"Why, Benny," I said, "I'd be glad to lend you the money, but if I do, I won't see you again for a year. Isn't that so?"

Benny laughed with great good nature.

"Yes, sir," he admitted candidly. "That's the truth, indeed it is."

"I don't want to lose you," I said. "You're a good hand. If I lend you this money, will you promise not to quit?"

"Land, Mister Colonel," Benny said, "you know I can't do that."

"Why not?"

Benny laughed again.

"I done made up my mind to quit," he said. "That's the only reason I'm asking you for the money."

In the beginning Benny was very helpful to Margaret. As he worked with Glee, Margaret would often go to a fence row they were weeding or a barn they were repairing, and talk to him. Benny is a great talker. Given an audience, he is expansive. He explained, in detail, the customs of the countryside, in such simple words that, like a jingling rhyme, they stuck in Margaret's memory.

He clammed up, though, the moment she asked any question that bore upon her relations with anyone who worked on the farm. Once Margaret attempted to extract from him, without his knowing it, some clues to a situation that arose, along toward autumn, with another member of the farm family, a tenant named Nelson.

Margaret and Nelson had been great friends. He was a man of considerable family, all the members of which were in constant physical pain or mental turmoil. At first he took his miseries to Margaret and she helped him to solve them. His overtures were oblique, of course. He would bring her a shirt that needed a button, or a sweater that was ripped, and ask her to repair it. Over the seamstress activity Nelson unburdened his soul.

One day Margaret became aware that Nelson was avoiding her. He began to send one of his many children to the house for his milk, a chore that formerly he had habitually undertaken. He ceased volunteering to reset logs in the fireplaces. And, amazingly, when one day she sought out Nelson and gave him the colloquial invitation to narrate his troubles by saying, "How you making, Nelson?" he had no burdens at all.

So Margaret knew something was wrong. She asked Glee about it. By his wary mien she sensed that Nelson was no longer happy on the farm and that Glee knew it, though he gave her no enlightenment as to the cause. Waylaying Benny then, Margaret adroitly, by generalization, drew him out concerning her obligations, as employer, to the tenants. Benny was delighted to oblige, and was just reaching an elaboration which Margaret thought might turn out to be helpful, when suddenly he appeared quite angry, and leaped to concealment behind a wall of silence. Something Margaret had said had tipped him off.

Benny was so indignant at this artful attempt to make him violate the code that sets off employer from employee that he did not come to work for a full week. Meanwhile, relations with Nelson did not improve.

About that time I came home for a day and Margaret put the problem of Nelson up to me. So far as I could tell, nothing was wrong. Nelson treated me politely, as usual, when I met him. He received good wages, his living conditions were standard, his findings above average. I decided to approach him directly.

"Nelson," I greeted him, "how are you getting along?"

"Tolerable."

"Any complaints?"

"No. I've been waiting some time for you to get here."

"What's on your mind?"

"I bargained to you, so I couldn't quit to the missus. I want you-all to know I'm leaving."

"Well, all right, if you want to," I said. "But if things aren't right, I'm prepared to make them right."

"No, I'll be going."

This was my first setback on the farm, and naturally I wanted to know what was wrong, lest I make the same mistake again. Nelson would give me no intelligible reason for his attitude. He admitted he did not have another job.

"Well, then, Nelson," I said, "surely we can iron this out. Just tell me the reason you're going."

He looked at me a moment, as though I should know without being told. Then he shook his head.

"It just don't suit," he said.

To him this was a definite answer. To me it meant nothing. Nowadays, faced with the same situation, I would look farther afield than material standards, for Virginia is still governed, to large extent, by the feudal system in agriculture. The wages are by no means feudal, but the carryover in attention to the spiritual needs of the family remains. Long ago, when first the slave, then the white or Negro hand, received little for his hire, his employer looked after him in many ways, took him to the doctor when he was ill, carried his children to Sunday School, patched up his quarrels with his wife, and jollied him along on blue days. These personal attentions were more important to the worker than his pay. When a hand says "It don't suit," he means that his employer did not make quite enough fuss over his indigestion, or perhaps give enough castoff clothes to his new baby. Visiting the farm infrequently, and not understanding the tradition, I lost a good hand for lack of personal attention.

That same autumn, along toward December, Margaret discovered that, due to improper planning and unthrifty feeding, our hogs would not be ready for December slaughter. Farm hands take part of their pay in pork. When the animals are slaughtered in the December cold snap, each hand receives, according to the bargain he has made, an allotment by weight of the pork as it hangs on the pole after disembowelment. Our bargains called for the distribution of six hundred pounds of pork. To go into the open market and buy fat hogs would have cost us one hundred and fifty dollars. In the feed lot, however, were some fattening steers.

Margaret proposed that, in lieu of pork, the hands take their quota in beef. To her this seemed a very fair trade, but the offer aroused no enthusiasm.

"Don't you want the beef?" she asked Glee.

"Well, yes," he replied hesitantly, "but what will we do for meat?"

To him, meat is something that may be salted, smoked, and preserved without refrigeration for use throughout the year. It also provides a generous rendering of lard. The entire farm diet is built around the pork ration. The wife of one of our workers makes bread, for example, by heating a skillet red hot on the stove, dropping into it a generous spoon of lard, adding a dash of salt, then throwing in quickly a mixture of white flour, baking soda, and water. When the paste rises into a hard dough, her bread is made. She makes and feeds it to her family thrice daily.

Pork also is the staple condiment for green vegetables. To all boiled greens, a little pork fat is added. The farm workers never eat greens raw. To them, "salad" means greens cooked with pork fat. Once Margaret took Glee's wife, Hazel, to the doctor after she complained of stomach cramps. A fresh leafy diet was prescribed. Margaret gave Hazel a head of lettuce, a head of cabbage, some hothouse tomatoes, and a jar of mayonnaise. The next day she inquired how Hazel liked the salad. "Why, it's all right," Hazel said dubiously, "but that mayonnaise don't boil up nice at all with the greens."

Slowly and cautiously Margaret felt her way through those first months, her letters becoming more confident as time went on. By autumn, when the winter oats were sown, and the arrival of her second child was upon her, she had begun to feel that she was making progress. She was not yet a part of the community. She was still an outsider, looking in, busy with her renovating, her baby, and many farm problems. But she knew now what the working people of the county were like, and that was a good start.

On one aspect of their life, however, she was still insecure. A strange occurrence had taken place on the farm that she could not place in relation to the whole. It concerned the morality of some of the farm hands. With four tenant houses occupied, she had neither the inclination nor the energy to be policeman, although she was aware that things were going on which possibly should have been her concern.

In particular she noticed that one of our tenant families, a prolific brood which increased annually, seemed to be the center of much ribaldry. A bit anxious, she consulted Glee who was delightfully evasive and suggested that perhaps she did not understand these things, a true understatement. Unwilling to offend against the customs of the countryside, yet by nature unable to condone such goings on within the limits of her own acres, she kept anxious watch on this particular house.

The family had a daughter who, about that time, began to wear sweaters self-consciously and otherwise indicate adolescence. A young man named Freddie, who wore a bright red hunting cap, began to carry her books from the school bus. One day a deputy sheriff, passing on the road in front of the farm, saw the red cap and investigated. The liaison he observed filled him with all the importance of the law. Home to mama he took the offending girl, the boy with her, and in a shocked voice described what he had seen.

The mother was not at all abashed.

"Mister sheriff," she said, "I will satisfy you to mind your own business. We poor folks likes it, and we starts young."

And so they do.

CHAPTER SEVEN

AFTER five months in the country, during all of which I was stationed in Washington, Margaret began to feel that she was getting somewhere. The premises no longer looked abandoned. The house had taken on a seedy respectability and the farm a shabby industry. The canning cupboard was filled with fruit and Margaret's heart with enthusiasm. All we needed, she wrote me in August, was a coat of paint on the house and the urgent improvements would be, for the moment, complete.

Progress had not been easy. At one stage, Margaret had canned peaches and pears until midnight for nearly a week, using corn syrup in lieu of war-scarce sugar. She then had sold the surplus orchard crop from the front lawn. This first venture in securing farm income had seemed like a good idea at the time. Margaret was quite jubilant when she advertised her wares in the weekly paper. The orchard had not been sprayed and the fruit was not of good quality. To offset this deficiency, Margaret spent two days carefully sorting the fruit and packing the best of it prettily in baskets. Three days later, when the first customer arrived, rot oozed from the bottom of the containers and Margaret had to re-sort three baskets to get one of salable quality. Not one to waste anything, Margaret shoveled the remainders into wheelbarrows and toted them to the pigs. She finally did sell eight bushels of peaches and two of pears, at a cost of thirty-two hours of her own labor, hardly an agreeable return. The experience taught her one lesson at least; namely, that marketing farm produce is likely to result in loss rather than gain. The principal loss involved, however, was indirect. In the fever of her merchandizing, Margaret forgot about a barrel of pears she had left on a hardwood floor near the kitchen to be canned when she found time. The pears rotted, spreading over the floor a wide stain which is still there, though hidden now beneath a scatter rug.

Fruit harvest out of the way, with the tangible asset of six hundred filled Mason jars in the basement, and fifteen dollars in cash, Margaret turned jubilantly to the living and dining rooms. They were disreputable, to say the least. Before their renovation, Margaret knew she must remove calcimine from the ceiling in both rooms, and wallpaper from one. Once she was down to bare walls, she could consider the problem of decoration. She called in Glee's son, Obed, and they went to work on the calcimine, anticipating a half day's swabbing with bucket and sponge. Calcimine, however, is stubborn stuff. At ten o'clock that night, with the dining room only half completed and the living room untouched, Margaret dismissed Obed, sat on the floor beside her bucket, and had a good cry. Her arms ached as from arthritis, her leg muscles trembled from overexertion all day on a shaky stepladder. Rallying finally, she decided to let Obed complete the scrubbing at his leisure. She would peel the florid red wallpaper from the living room. Happier at this prospect, she went to the living room for a tentative exploration of the task before her. In a few minutes she was crying again. Instead of an easy stripping of paper long mildewed and rotten, as in the hall, she faced four coats of wallpaper, each glued on with some unorthodox but effective adhesive. The only way to get it off was to scrape it laboriously, one coat at a time. Even here, however, there was one optimistic note. The dining room wallpaper, a fine old English print, was perfectly preserved and needed no replacement at all.

Summer's end found the living and dining rooms tentatively overhauled. At least they were clean at last, an oil paint covered the living-room walls and hall walls until such postwar time as permanent improvements could be made, and the dining room, embellished with new rose and gold draperies, was acceptable if not elegant. A week of labor had removed the crank case oil from all the floors. Now, if any neighbor should be disposed to call, Margaret thought, she was ready, provided she could prevent the guest from wandering farther than the two front rooms.

Glee likewise had been busy. The front lawn was pleasantly green. Tons of rock, gathered in cleaning up the fields, had been cracked with a mallet and used to fortify the driveway. A sawmill had moved in and cut twelve thousand feet of white oak into fence strips with which Glee and Benny had constructed a plank fence along the entire front of the property facing the county road.

Margaret's jubilation over this progress was evident to me in a letter which reported: "We are on our way at last. All the immediate repairs are done, and the house painters have at last hinted that they may arrive next week. When the painting is done, our worries are over and the place will be in pretty good shape."

Then the seasonal rains began. Going one morning to the basement for a can of wild raspberries she had put up, Margaret stepped into two feet of water, which cascaded the full length of the floor and out the cellar door. Donning

69

rubber boots, she investigated. The basement was only half underground, its many windows sunk in wells to let in light. Water pouring from leaky eaves spilled into these wells, filling them, and the water, having nowhere to go, splashed through rotted sills. Stronger cataracts suggested even more serious trouble from four freshets that rippled, like vigorous springs, through the house foundation. For a week after the rain ended, the basement was sodden, and the upstairs so damp that door frames swelled and scarcely a door would close. Closet doors, of course, would not open.

After this flood had subsided, Margaret searched the basement carefully. She had cause to regret her optimistic letter of the previous week, for here, indeed, was a major disorder. Ceiling beams were rotted to such an extent that the floor overhead threatened to come down, particularly where it supported such heavy objects upstairs as the refrigerator, radio, and piano. Glee placed temporary props under the critical weaknesses, and Margaret turned to a clean page in her desk pad and inscribed the basement condition in detail under the bold caption: TROUBLE!!!

Other entries followed. Plaster fell from the ceiling in one wing, disclosing an unsound roof. Some years earlier, it seemed, a large oak tree had crashed across the roof during a storm, opening every seam in the metal covering. Nothing had been done to repair it and now the rafters and sheeting were rotting away.

Next, Margaret lay in bed one night during a lightning storm, unable to sleep from worry over the staggering repair bills she would receive from work in the basement and on the roof, when she saw an arc of electricity leap a fifteen-inch gap between two sockets in a chandelier. She recalled what the plumber had said about our faulty fuse receptacle, and immediately arose and added this item to her list, lest she forget it again. While she was at it, she penned a description of the sagging front porch, which was slipping gradually down the big pillars at the front of the house, causing the tongue-and-grove flooring to buckle nearly an inch just before the front door.

Glee reported the next entry for "Trouble!!!" The main barn was a structure one hundred and twenty feet long by fifty wide, with a cavernous hay floor and grain bins on its upper side, and feeding space for cattle underneath. The uprights looked substantial, being twelve inches square, but Glee, tentatively testing them with a jackknife, discovered that they were made of pine which was feeding millions of wood-boring worms. He had put up what hay the farm grew that summer, and had baled a straw stack. The weight of all this feed caused the barn to creak and shudder in the least wind.

The same day, Glee came back again, most regretfully. Fixing a chimney flashing on his house, he had found a huge crack in the chimney. His cook stove had been connected to this chimney all summer, and only a miracle had kept the house from burning down. Glee said he guessed the roof timbers were just too rotten to burn.

How the farm had been allowed to disintegrate was a testimonial to the common American practice of living off the land without any thought to the future. Our acreage had once been known far and wide as "the best farm in the county." It had been developed by a man named Dietrich who, in addition to being a good farmer, had also been in the commercial fertilizer business. He had used the farm to demonstrate what proper treatment could do to increase the abundance of the soil. His yields of crops had been far above the county average, and his pastures had supported more cattle per acre than those of his neighbors.

71

He had lived in a fine old frame house, painted yellow, on a hilltop facing the broad panorama of the Blue Ridge Mountains which brought forty miles of valley into his front yard. It was he who had built the big barns and tenant buildings.

Then the farm had been acquired along with two hundred acres of hardwood timber by an adjacent neighbor, a millionaire, for his son. The great house in which we live had been built as a home for the young man and his bride. Extensive improvements again had been made, a brick machine shed constructed, and an elaborate stable for carriage horses. The parks and gardens had been developed, the swimming pool and tennis court installed. A great herd of Hereford cattle enjoyed the land, deer and bison added a decorative note to the front pastures, and behind the house, in a pen, had lived four cinnamon bears. The county hotbloods, seeking amusement, would slip over on Saturday night and let the bears out into the adjacent woods, knowing that their master would raise a hue and cry in the morning for help to get them back. Already saddled, bridled, and dressed when the alarm was spread, the young men would rally to the hunt and spend Sunday morning in exciting sport. Legend reports that the master of Gaston Hall never did discover how his bears had been loosed. He had built the fences ever higher and higher, until today they stand up twenty feet, heavily reinforced with wire and stout planks. Gaston Hall was a showplace in those days.

The land fell, by inheritance, into the hands of an outlander. Now for the first time tragedy dimmed the sun over the farm's great acres. Whether this man, whom we shall call Sheldon, had no love of the land or whether World War I, in which he fought as an artillery major, had left scars upon him, is not clear. County memories, as so often in such cases, are both confused and prejudiced. The family which had built Gaston Hall was much loved and honored. Sheldon did not maintain the tradition.

At first the county, in true Virginia fashion, gave him opportunity to become one of them, for he was an illustrious personage. A trial lawyer of such note that his cases were textbook examples of procedure in law schools, he had been highly esteemed in his native New England. He was connected, professionally and through friendship, to several county families who introduced him and his teenage daughter to the community. While this daughter was at Gaston Hall, Sheldon made a show of maintaining the premises in elaborate style, though one by one his friendships came to an end until, after the daughter's marriage, most county doors were closed to her father. What he had done to deserve this ostracism again is not clear. The great herd of cattle was dispersed. A tenant invaded the land. The gardens grew to sorry weeds. Sheldon's practice of law ended, for lack of custom. And he, surrounded by a few cronies from far away, added daily to the pile of empty whisky bottles outside the back door. The bear, the elk, the bison disappeared; starved to death, the county thinks.

This degradation culminated in the filing of two tax liens against the premises. Now Sheldon tried to sell, but his grandiose ideas of the worth of his shabby establishment reflected its former estate, not its current condition. Perhaps, in his alcoholic fog, he still saw Gaston Hall as it had been, not as it was. Perhaps when he stood on the back porch, glass in hand, he still saw banked on a gentle rise the eight hundred rosebushes that once had been there. He must not have noticed the checked paint, the leaking roofs, the

73

flooded basement, the wilderness of weeds, for surely some sentimentality, if nothing more, would have stirred in him a little pride and an urge to rise above his ruin.

Unable to sell, Sheldon for a number of years milked a paltry existence from his acres. How he managed to survive, no one knows, though there are clues. A colored man who once worked here told me that his uncle had been Sheldon's tenant farmer. This uncle received a legacy of five hundred dollars. Sheldon heard about it.

"Willis," he said, "what are you doing with all that money you inherited?"

"Why, Mr. Sheldon, sir, it's in the bank. That's my burying money."

"You aren't getting much interest on it."

"Three per cent."

"I tell you, Willis," Sheldon reputedly said, "I like you, and I want to help you. You loan me that money, and I'll give you twelve per cent."

Willis obliged. Sheldon paid the interest once. When the next due date came round, Sheldon is said to have exclaimed, "Why man, I don't owe you any money. You are charging me usurious interest. That's against the law. Sue me, if you don't believe me, and see how far you get in court."

Willis died not long after, and his family buried him. He left behind, at the yellow frame farmhouse, two police dogs which, when we arrived, were still here awaiting the return of their master.

However he lived, Sheldon could not go on that way forever. When Willis died, Sheldon was unable to find a tenant anywhere. No one would work for him. Somehow, again this is not clear, his divorced wife gained title to the property, paid off the liens to clear the title, and offered Gaston Hall for sale. Again the price was too high. Finally, weary of paying mortgage interest and taxes on a slowly rotting establishment to which Sheldon still clung, although now he had moved into a single unheated room, the wife put the place up at auction, and Margaret and I acquired it.

On the day of the sale, Sheldon stood on the front porch, glass in hand as usual, and watched the proceedings. He looked out haughtily over the large crowd, as though he was still the master of a great estate. He was a little man with a large head sparsely covered with white hair. The marks of drink were upon him; his eyes were bloodshot, his nose swollen and pitted. Definitely he was a part of all the deterioration visible throughout the house and grounds; he complemented it perfectly.

Even now he did not seem to realize to what destruction he had brought the farm. When the hammer fell, he wept openly. Then, returning to the library which had been his home, he poured another generous slug from his bottle, downed it, and put his hands on my shoulders.

"I love Gaston Hall," he said thickly but apparently sincerely; "be good to it."

He went up north after he left this place. I was not surprised to read in the paper, not long afterward, that he had died. If ever a man committed suicide, it was he. And he did it the hardest way of all, by strangling his soul to death.

The history of the farm impressed upon Margaret and me the fact that the land can break, as well as make, the individual who lives on it and with it. But the deep significance of this truth did not affect us personally for another two years. Then we were able to understand poor old Sheldon better. But more of that in its proper place.

Sheldon had not even had a telephone. During our first summer the absence of telephonic communication probably saved us from bankruptcy, as Margaret would have been telephoning me in Washington every night with some new problem that had arisen. Somehow, when she committed her troubles to a letter, they lost the sharp edge of urgency as other, and more disastrous burdens, overtook her.

By autumn the telephone was a necessity. Since Lampert had been born in New York, and had cost a pretty penny, we had decided to reduce our natal investment by getting Laurie free, courtesy of the Army Air Corps. This necessitated Margaret's appearance at Bolling Field at the proper moment.

Expecting the house painters, however, Margaret refused to leave the farm. She had heard too many stories about the originality of Virginia craftsmen when left to themselves. A neighbor, for example, having inherited two fine coach lamps and two French crystal candelabra, called in workmen to electrify them and hang them, one set on the front porch, the other in her bedroom. She was not at home when the work was done. Returning, she found the delicate crystals bobbing in the wind on the front porch and the great coach lamps astride the fireplace mantel upstairs. Lest the painters make the dormer sky blue and the porch ceiling pure white, Margaret wanted to be on the job herself. I consented to this only if a telephone was installed.

In the city you call the service department and the next day a man connects your phone. Margaret called the local company manager, but he did not appear the next day. Instead, he sent her a written request for a war priority, and several alternate proposals. She could be on a twelve-party or an eight-party circuit, provided that we bought and set up, at our own expense, a mile and a quarter of telephone poles. Margaret declined to accept this. She had heard too much talk about party wires. One of her acquaintances had abandoned all attempts to fight her way onto the line before

76

ten o'clock at night, and communicated with friends and business people after all the inquisitive line sharers had retired for the night. Margaret held out for a private line. Meanwhile she could get none at all, even a congested rural wire, without a "certificate of necessity," due to war restrictions.

Here, the Air Corps helped me handsomely. My general agreed with me that, since I visited my farm on occasion and thus was "out of touch," a telephone at the farm was necessary. Since military business might thus be transacted between my general and me, a private wire was mandatory.

The local telephone manager arose to his war duty, and found a way. A circuit he had not previously mentioned became available, provided my neighbor would allow me to extend a line of ten poles across one of his crop fields. This consent was obtained, and Glee went hunting for poles.

Meanwhile the painters arrived, and Margaret saw within a day that the work would exceed her budget by at least fifty per cent. One of the largest items in the estimate concerned two balustrades which ran about the top of the wings. These ornaments had not been painted for twenty years, and a scabrous scale, partially peeled, a holdover from the checking of many years, required scraping before the wood could be painted. The painters wanted two hundred dollars to clean off the railings, and Margaret balked. The telephone line, the leaky basement, and the wing roof, all very expensive items, were on her mind as she told the painters, "Nonsense. I'll get up there myself and scrape those things, and you come back next spring and paint them."

Unfortunately she was in no condition to struggle up an extension ladder to the rooftop. So when the painters ended their work, the house did not look painted at all. The balustrades, stretching out for sixty feet on each side

77

of the main house, gave the entire structure a shabby appearance.

The telephone line was completed on the day the painters left. By that time Margaret was ready to leave the farm for the winter. The phone was not used once until the following spring.

Margaret and Lampert took up residence in their old cigar box in Washington, which I still occupied, and, as usual in times of stress, Stella paid us a visit. This time her husband, Doctor Linn, remembering his long summer alone, came along too.

I was in a staff meeting one morning discussing, as I recall, the deployment of the big B-29 bombers against the mainland of Japan for the first time, when my aide popped his head in the door and, aware that to interrupt a General's staff meeting was very much like disrupting the Mass, broke quaveringly upon the General's discourse.

"Beg pardon, sir," he said, saluting as befits a second lieutenant just up from officers' training, "but Mrs. Spence says that if the colonel doesn't get home quick she'll have to bail out without help from the Medical Corps."

The General looked puzzled.

"We are expecting a baby, sir," I mumbled meekly from my place at the foot of the table. I sat at the foot because I was the lowest ranking member.

"Very well, you are excused."

Being a veteran of this sort of thing, I did not hurry. I stopped for gasoline, mindful of the twelve-mile ride across Washington that was before me. When I reached home I discovered that I had timed my arrival badly. The doctor, not I, should have been making his entrance at this point.

Margaret, Stella, and Grandpa piled tensely into the car and away we went. Grandpa, who is a dentist and thus has at least an associate knowledge of physiology, sat in the back seat, his watch in hand, his eyes on Margaret. Clearly there was no time to lose.

I swung onto the boulevard and put the footfeed to the floor. Stella was grim, for her an unusual state, and I could not tell whether the wild ride or the calisthenics on my right was the cause of it. Ordinarily, one need go only two miles over the speed limit on Sherley Boulevard to pick up a police escort, but today, one hand on the horn, I hit the Fourteenth Street bridge—a fifteen-mile-an-hour zone—at seventy, scattering trucks and taxicabs to right and left, and not a policeman appeared. I prayed for the police to catch me speeding. They did not respond. I did not know then that Tuesday morning they are all in traffic court.

Like a fire engine we slashed through traffic lights and wore out our precious tires on curves while Grandpa, gripping his watch ever more firmly, advised me, "You'd better step on it, son," and Stella kept repeating over and over, like a wire recording on an endless tape, "Don't kill us all, now."

At Bolling Field we dispersed the gate guards with a blast of the horn, and sped up the runway apron to the back door of the hospital. Margaret was hurried inside and I, seeing two military police jeeps rounding a corner, decided to get out of there. I returned to my staff meeting, which was still in progress.

The General raised his eyebrows at this new interruption, but said nothing. The problem under discussion was intricate, involving the transportation of the sixteen thousand spare parts for the B-29 to bases on Saipan from which the mainland of Japan might be reached. I was just nicely settled in my chair when the telephone at the General's elbow rang softly.

Here was another sacrilege. Staff meetings are interrupted

only by the summons of very high authority, and since our General was important himself, he assumed that his call must be from the Chief of Staff. Crisply he seized the receiver and barked a well-disciplined "Yes, sir." Margaret answered him. She wanted to talk to her husband. Clearly, even from the foot of the table, I heard her voice, as did all the illustrious generals present. She had begged her way onto the conference-room line by insisting that her message was one of life or death.

So it was, of life.

"It's a girl," she said, as I, at the General's elbow while the staff discussion waited, felt the heat rising to the top of my head. "Aren't you glad?"

"Yes, dear," I said, meekly.

"What did you say?"

"I said, 'Yes, dear.' "

"Aren't you gladder than that?"

"Yes, dear."

"Well, you certainly don't sound like it."

"No, really I am, but . . ."

"I saw the whole thing. It was wonderful."

She then explained, at considerable length, how her arrival at the hospital had preceded that of her daughter by only two minutes, and therefore she had been a witness to the miracle. She had then insisted on telephoning to me, and the hospital staff had humored her whim.

The General stirred remindfully and I interrupted. "I'll be over this afternoon," I said quickly. "Good-by, now," and I disconnected.

There was deep silence as I returned to the foot of the table. General Norstad's eyes, I saw in passing, were breaking out in laughter, though not a muscle twitched on his rigid face. Another general, who fortunately had nothing to do with me, appeared to be approaching apoplexy. Still another, with whom I had always been on the best of terms, wore a pensive expression as though trying to remember where, on the morning report, he had seen a request from an obscure post in Greenland or the Aleutians for one lieutenant colonel, in grade.

The big boss meanwhile waited until I was seated. Fixing me then with a searing stare, he appeared to await an explanation.

"It's a girl, sir," I mumbled.

The general's mien did not relax.

"So we heard," he said. "Shall we get on with the war?"

CHAPTER EIGHT

LAURIE'S birth inaugurated a tumult
that continued until after the Christmas holidays. She
brought home from the hospital a case of colic that set her
to crying immediately after her eight p.m. feeding with a
persistence that prevailed until daylight.

Simultaneously, air operations in the Pacific were put on
a twenty-four-hour-a-day schedule, which necessitated my
presence in the Pentagon almost round the clock. No matter at what hour of the day or night I sped home for a few
hours rest, I found the place in turmoil. By day, Lampert
expressed his jealousy over the addition to the family, and
by night the colicky newcomer wailed continuously.

The cigar-box apartment was a fit setting for such bed-
lam. It had hardly been large enough for Margaret, Lampert,
and me, and now was swollen with the addition of Laurie,
Stella, and Dr. Linn. My bed, when I was in the house, was
a studio couch in the front room. All traffic from upstairs
to the kitchen went past my head, and this thoroughfare was
in use at all hours.

Along about the fifth day, my father-in-law expressed the
common sentiment of us all.

"This is no place for me," he said, threw his luggage into

his Studebaker, and headed for Nebraska. Stella remained on, under promise to follow him in a fortnight.

Many a night I came in about four a.m., under compulsion to be back at work in time for a nine a.m. staff meeting, to find Stella or Margaret sitting on the top stairstep with howling Laurie in her lap, while in the one bedroom Lampert and an exhausted woman were asleep. About the time Laurie quieted down, Lampert was up for the day, Stella and Margaret changed shifts, and I, trying to sleep below, was caught between breakfast preparations in the kitchen and Lampert swarming over me ready to play games. In desperation finally, defeated by the Battle of the Babies, I set up a cot in the Pentagon and went home only to shave and change clothes. This gave relief to me but none to Margaret, for after Stella departed, Margaret had no help. Entering the house one morning about six o'clock for a quick bath before returning to duty, I found Margaret asleep in a chair, Laurie in her arms still complaining of colic. There were tears on the baby's forehead, as well as on her cheeks.

This went on all through October and November and into December, while the Air Corps devised no formula to relieve me of my continuous labors or the pediatrician a diet that would end Laurie's crying.

By Christmas time even the army could see I was whipped, for I fell asleep one morning in staff meeting. I was given a fifteen-day leave. I hurried to the apartment.

"Let's go down to the farm," I suggested. "At least there's peace and quiet there. We can spread out; everyone with a room to himself. We'll get a nursemaid to take care of Lampert and I'll spell you with Laurie, and we'll both get some rest."

"How about the furnace?" Margaret asked. "You've never tried to make it work."

"It's got to work," I said. "Come on, let's pack."

The excitement of spending our first Christmas on our own acres and the prospect of fifteen days of relaxation made us forget, in an instant, the previous cruel months. In gala mood we drove to the farm. The weather was windy and cold. Snow, rare in our countryside, lay six inches deep on the ground, covering the weedy fields and adorning the big brick house with stately elegance.

The water had been shut off, of course, the system drained, and all vulnerable traps filled with kerosene. While I set about making the house livable, Margaret and the children searched the snow-adorned woods for a Christmas tree. Lampert now was old enough to walk a little, and Laurie got in the spirit of the occasion by giggling and gurgling from the baby carriage in which Margaret hauled her into the forest.

On their return, the house was not warm. Instead, it was full of smoke. The old boiler would not work. Years of rust clogged the pipes and sealed the air vents in the radiators. The chimney, heavy with soot and swallows' nests, would not draw. The house, with its thick brick walls, was damp as well as cold.

Hurriedly I rigged a wood stove in the library fireplace. Soon the room was unbearably hot, but at least it was a change from the previous cold. Outside that one room, the house was untenantable. To venture into the hall, or up-stairs to a bedroom was to encounter a penetrating iciness far worse than the dry cold of the outdoors.

"We'll each have a room to ourselves," Margaret laughed as we decided to utilize the library alone rather than to return to the apartment, "and peace and quiet."

We set up the fir tree in a corner and Margaret began to decorate it while Lampert, excited by the spirit of Christmas, picked the fragile glass ornaments from their boxes and

84

hurled them one by one against the mantel. Curbed of this enthusiasm, he investigated the strands of glittering tinsel, denuding them of their shining antennae and leaving them barren strings. Undaunted, Margaret popped popcorn over the wood stove, strung it on strings, and hung it on the tree while Lampert made havoc with the cotton pads which had been set at the base of the tree to hide its iron stand behind simulated snow. All this time I was busy carrying cots, electric plates, dishes, and sundries into the library, so that the room might serve as living quarters, bedroom, boudoir, dining room, and kitchen. The tree adorned and lighted, we gathered about the heating stove, happier than we had been since midsummer, to savor the aroma of pork sausage and eggs frying in a skillet. All this time Laurie slept peacefully in her buggy, even through the singing of carols and the blare of a radio.

Finally turning off the Christmas tree lights and banking the fire, we settled contentedly to sleep, snug in our own home—such as it was—and contemplating with gusto the delicious relaxation that awaited us during two weeks in the country. My last conscious action was to look about from my creaking cot at my family bedded for the night, peering in turn, over the red glowlight of the stove, at Lampert, whose blond curls gave him an angelic appearance; at Laurie, the tip of whose nose alone was uncovered; at Margaret, relaxed in sleep on her own cot nearby; and finally at the gala Christmas tree and the mantel from which dangled four stockings to catch the bounty of Santa Claus. The peace of Christmas settled over my house.

Then Laurie began to cry, resuming her nightly protest against improper feeding. Quickly, lest Lampert waken, I picked her up. Unaccustomed to my ministrations, she made altogether plain that she wanted her mother. I was only too happy to relinquish her to Margaret, and Laurie then settled down to a routine of fussing and fighting her aching tummy. She did not exactly cry. She would whimper a little, gasp as though she were strangling, wave her little fists wildly, cluck angrily, let out one rousing whoop, and then subside again to a whimper. All this time she squirmed like a baby pig as her legs and arms reacted spasmodically to her intestinal rebellion.

"This is stupid," I groaned to Margaret along about two in the morning when, for a moment, Laurie had quieted down sufficiently to drink some warm milk. "Here we have a baby three months old and she is still fighting her feed. Surely that high-priced pediatrician can do something for her."

"He's trying," Margaret said wearily. "He has changed her formula five times."

"Then try a sixth."

"He will, if this one doesn't work."

"And then a seventh, I suppose?" I said tartly.

"She'll probably just have to outgrow it," Margaret said. She was too weary to argue the point.

"At what age, for goodness sake?" I said.

"About a year. Then she'll be on Pablum and cereals, and whatever is troubling her will probably take care of itself."

"Maybe," I said, "we should just start the Pablum and cereals tomorrow. We'll both be dead of nervous exhaustion before the year is up."

Margaret just looked at me, as does a mother when her husband has made an inane comment about bringing up a baby. No, plainly this was a cross that had to be borne. It was one of those terrible trials that makes a mother love her child the more.

86

Laurie seemed quieter now, so Margaret lay down and I carried on alone. Two long hours passed. Laurie was perverse. She would lie happily grinning at me, thoroughly awake and playful, until I began to doze. The moment my head drooped and my eyes closed, she whooped and went into her whimpering, gasping, and squirming, and Margaret would wake and raise her head.

"Just a spoiled brat," I told myself over and over. "If we'd just let her cry this thing out once—just once—we'd cure her. I don't think there's anything wrong with her tummy at all."

I must have said this aloud at least once, for Margaret opened her eyes at one point and, as though cued by my utterance replied, "Oh, yes there is!"—and went back to sleep.

Dawn was preparing its entrance over the tips of the pine trees behind the house when Laurie finally went to sleep. I tiptoed to my cot and lay down. Before I had even arranged my blanket, I heard a sound that threw me out of bed in a jump.

"Cah-rump!" It was something like that, and it seemed to have come from Lampert. He was perfectly still. I lay down again.

"Cah-rump!" This time the sound unmistakably had come from my son. I went to him. His brow was moist with fever. He tossed, articulated again his piercing cough. This time I diagnosed the sound. He had the croup.

Doctors tell me that no child has ever yet died of croup. This is no reassurance to a parent who suddenly, before dawn on Christmas Day, with the baby's pediatrician a hundred miles away, watches his son tear himself apart in the agonies of coughing. Within a matter of minutes Lampert seemed in imminent danger of choking to death, and again Margaret arose from her bed. We did what we could do, gave Lampert

87

half an aspirin and tucked him in warmly, and had just decided to abandon further attempts to sleep when, from Laurie's crib came a piping miniature of her brother's voice.

"Cah-rump!" she wheezed.

This woke Lampert.

Christmas was not a happy day. Margaret and I huddled about the fire, I holding Lampert, she nursing Laurie. We left the warm room only as urgent demands fell upon us. We did not even try to find a nursemaid. Four persons in one small room were enough. After dark, Laurie's stomach cramps began again.

By the dawn of December 26th, Margaret and I were defeated. Bundling the children into the car, we sped back to the steam-heated cigar box and the pediatrician. The children were no sooner in their own beds than they settled down to catch up on their sleep—and so did the parents.

I proposed to spend the rest of my leave helping Margaret, but she would not hear of it. The army had told me to rest, she reminded me, and suggested I go back to the farm alone.

We made a deal. I would take my rest now, and in the spring, as soon as she returned to the farm where household help was more plentiful, she would leave the children with a nurse and spend a fortnight in New York. Margaret accepted this compromise enthusiastically. I returned to the farm and pruned trees for ten days while Margaret carried on with the children.

Until the first week in March, Laurie's colic continued. Finally Margaret telephoned me at the Pentagon, saying I could abandon my cot. A new formula had done wonders for Laurie. She had enjoyed two nights of uninterrupted sleep.

The day was warm and for once I had nothing to do, due to a typhoon that had disrupted operations in the Pacific.

We drove to the farm. The forsythia was just breaking out, snowflowers and hyacinths were abloom in the side yard. Winter had vanished.

Margaret, stretching her care-worn body in the warming sun, decided that she and the children would stay. She found a nursemaid before the day ended, and began to make plans for her trip to New York.

I returned to the Pentagon. On my desk was a note.

"Report to Walter Reed Hospital 0800 for routine physical examination."

I went. And there I stayed.

The doctors took one look at me and tossed me into the psychiatric ward.

CHAPTER NINE

I LANGUISHED in the hospital while Margaret postponed her trip to New York from day to day and finally deferred it indefinitely. She let me feel the irony of our situation by letter, however, pointing out the oddity that I, who had had fifteen days of rest, had gone to the hospital while she, after four months of twenty-four-hour schedules, was hale enough to undertake another summer of farming and baby tending.

Naturally, I had expected to be back at work in a few days. The corn was planted, the first hay crop cut, and the oats harvested while I worked jigsaw puzzles, swallowed benzedrine, and submitted to interminable interviews from army psychiatrists who told me all their troubles. I began to suspect, and Margaret to fear, that I was not in a hospital at all, but in an insane asylum.

The most awkward part of the situation in which I found myself was that I was out of contact with the farm. The doctors would not let me go home and Margaret, almost convinced of my insanity, began to couch her letters in benzedrine tones, studiously phrased to censor all farm problems and thus maintain my composure.

During the first weeks, I heard through the grapevine that the Medical Corps suspected me of malingering, of simulating the symptoms of permanent disability so I might retire on a tax-free life pension. I kicked that one in the head at my next psychiatric interview.

"I understand," I said, "that you jokers think I'm malingering."

"Well, now," the captain answered, "you mustn't worry about what we think or don't think is wrong with you. You just relax until we find out."

"If malingering implies that there is nothing wrong with me," I pursued the issue, "I will agree with you. The only thing I'm suffering from is boredom. If I never see another jigsaw puzzle or Grey Lady I'll be a happy man."

This evidently was the wrong approach, for the next day they gave me the full investigation for stomach ulcers. This is a most unpleasant technique involving a proctoscope, and I knew it was a punishment for talking up. For the next two weeks I said nothing at all, and the grapevine brought the intelligence that I now suffered from chronic moodiness and preoccupation and was beginning to develop acute symptoms of involutional melancholia. I took no interest in life, they said, and might even be developing a will to die. What they didn't know was that, to save myself from ennui, I was hiding out all day in the chaplain's office writing the script for a half-hour weekly network radio show based on my book *One Foot in Heaven*. I reported to the medical department only as often as summoned, and the floor orderly, mighty obliging for five dollars a week, warned me, in plenty of time, of the approach of medical dignitaries. This writing produced considerable revenue, which went week by week to the farm, where it was put to good use in such capital improvements as a new electric pump (at the barn, not at the house, over which Margaret burned for a week although she would not upset me by disputing the subject), new roofs for several buildings, and some farm machinery.

That second summer the farm outgrew its weeds. But the extensive tillage of five hundred acres of cropland and pasture, particularly on such a neglected tract where putting each field into production necessitated a hundred hours of ditching, tiling, fencing, and soil improvement, was a job for a professional farmer and six assistants, not a city-bred woman with two babies, a willing but unschooled foreman, and such other help as could be recruited in a labor-starved community. Margaret plowed, baled hay and straw, and ran the mower, tended a vegetable garden, canned hundreds of quarts of fruit and other produce, and kept the lawn mowed. Often she worked in the fields while Lampert played along the fence row and Laurie napped in a station wagon parked within eye range. From time to time she secured household help, only to lose it to a war factory within a few weeks.

Although I did not know it until later, she was having troubles that the writers of agricultural pamphlets apparently never encounter.

There was, for example, the strange case of Horatio, the Angus bull. The previous autumn, when we had sold the steers, I had bought a herd of purebred Angus cows. They were not the best cows in the state of Virginia, by any means, but I did not know that at the time. On paper they were wonderful. Then it says here in the book that the farm bull must be a good animal. He must be superior to the cow herd, so that the annual calf crop will be an improvement over the cows. The implication is that if you stay in business long enough, selling off your old cows and keeping your choice heifers, you will one day be breeding nothing but perfect animals, and the world will wear out your front road trying to buy them at any price. So I had attended a purebred sale and had bought the champion of the show. Nothing but the best, I said.

This bull was a handsome fellow, fat, sleek, and tractable. However, as Margaret discovered that spring, he did not

do his work. With a harem of tempting females vying for his attention, Horatio, like Munro Leaf's Ferdinand, sat on a hilltop admiring the daisies, the bluegrass, and the mountain view. Two gallons of grain a day he consumed with aplomb, in addition to the best pasture, yet he was not lord and master of the herd. His mother had not told him anything. Needless to say, Margaret made other arrangements, but by that time the farm had lost a half year's production and the calving schedules were six months in arrears.

Then there were the five sows. I had been negotiating for a purebred boar, on the same principle of the supremacy of the sire. The hospital seized me before the deal was completed, so all spring there was no porcine male on the farm. In some immaculate manner those sows presented Margaret with the most insulting litters of runt pigs ever seen outside the hills of Georgia. To offset this barnyard skullduggery, Margaret purchased two piggy sows of high repute and high price. Both aborted.

About that time, too, our most expensive cow broke through the fence onto the railroad track and was killed. The main line of a railroad cuts through our property. For twenty years it had been under no compulsion to repair the fences adjacent to us. I had been conducting, in high legal phrases, some correspondence with the railroad on this subject, without result. Instead of strengthening the fences, the section crew had completely rebuilt, from the ground, a bridge that crossed the tracks between our house and the main road, but there had been nothing wrong with this bridge. After the cow's demise, Margaret discovered an old law which permitted landowners abutting railroads to close the right of way if claims for damages were not settled within sixty days. She threatened to close the road, and a new fence promptly was built and, incidentally, the deceased cow paid for.

All this was nerve-racking for her, coming as it did on top of a heavy schedule of farm work and baby tending. Naturally, she could not watch everything. A carpenter, hired to roof a tenant house, used the precious lumber and even more precious nails to build a porch, on the excuse that

94

he was afraid of heights. A colt, which was to have been sold within a few days, ruptured himself in a tangle of old fencing wire that had been carelessly left in a pasture. The combine was not cleaned after the oats harvest, and rats chewed beyond repair its canvas conveyor. No replacement was procurable at any price.

I did not discover these things until July, when Margaret paid me a visit. Then I roared like a bull (not Horatio) to get out of the hospital. This is not easy to do. Anyone in uniform may get into a military hospital if he stands in line long enough outside the receiving room, but to be discharged is another matter. I suspect that the reason for this is that the commandant's rank depends on the number of beds occupied, and he is afraid to discharge a patient lest he empty his wards and be bumped from his war-inflated temporary brigadier generalship to his permanent grade of first lieutenant. After a week of insistence that my case be diagnosed or I be returned to duty, I was truly a psychiatric case and the army took cognizance of my alarming rise in metabolism by scheduling an appearance for me before the retirement board, an evidence that I was incurable. Since this met only bimonthly and had just adjourned, I had two weeks to wait. At this news I boarded a streetcar, went across town, and begged assistance from General Norstad.

"There's nothing wrong with me that getting out of that bughouse won't cure," I told him, "but that psychiatric business is contagious. I'm slowly going nuts."

The general investigated. Evidently something was wrong with me, because the best he could do was to bail me out of Walter Reed and send me to a de luxe rest camp for combat-wounded pilots up in New York State. So I wound up farther from the farm than ever.

The day of victory in Europe was celebrated. At home

the hay was in the barn, except for an autumn legume called lespedeza, and the fields were being ordered for winter wheat and barley. From Margaret's letters, all was well. There was no trouble, nothing to upset me. As for me, I was living, like a valuable herd sire, in clover up to my knees, with food comparable to that served at an expensive summer resort. The psychiatrist left me alone in my private cottage overlooking a lake, except for a morning visit each day after breakfast when, with a retinue of nurses and flunkies, he popped his head in my door, shouted "Any complaints?" and hurried away before I could make any. He had laid down an embargo on any writing, however, and the officer of the day carried out his orders so literally that I had difficulty composing letters to Margaret.

"Just loaf," were my orders.

I am not by nature an idler. Nothing so fatigues me as inactivity. I began to visit farms in the neighborhood, and to follow a veterinarian on his calls, to pick up what knowledge might be handy to me once I returned to the farm.

The atom bomb dropped on Hiroshima and the next day I was ordered to Mitchel Field for separation. The psychiatrist was quite nice about it.

"I'm sorry we had to keep you so long," he said. "You've been ill, make no mistake about that, but you've been ready to leave here for quite a while. Evidently you knew some secret and they couldn't let you out for fear you'd talk during an irrational moment."

"I thought maybe that was it," I said. "I was in the Twentieth Air Force, and that's the outfit that dropped the atom bomb."

"I see," said the psychiatrist.

"Do you know what really drove me nuts?" I asked, relieved at last to be free to talk.

The psychiatrist beamed, and begged me to answer the question.

"I've never been able to keep a secret in my life," I said, "and this time I had to. I couldn't even tell my wife about it. Well—I'll be all right now."

"There's just one more thing," the psychiatrist said, gravely. "You are not being retired on pay."

"Oh, that's all right," I said. "Just let me out of this jail and I can take care of myself."

"Don't be so sure," he said. "I doubt you will ever write again. Don't even try for a while. Build yourself back slowly. Give yourself a year, at least. Then perhaps you can go back to work."

"All I want is to get to my farm. You're delaying me," I said.

The psychiatrist smiled and let me go.

The farm looked beautiful, tidy, and shipshape. But the cost of this beauty was an expenditure of Margaret's own youth and stamina. Her great brown eyes were shadowed, her body shrunken and weary. She was twenty pounds lighter than when I had last seen her, and she was very near nervous exhaustion.

I wasted no time taking charge.

"Oh, no," I admonished her as from long habit she prepared to board the truck for a day of field work, "not any more. That's my job now. You go in and pack your bags. You're leaving for New York tonight for a vacation."

Her face came out from under a cloud.

"You mean it!" she exclaimed.

"It's an order," I said.

That afternoon, salvaging some grain sacks, I snapped a corner of one sack into my right eye. Margaret took me to the hospital, where I remained two days.

Margaret's trip, scheduled anew a week later, was postponed a second time by the arrival of her brother for a visit. Bud had just been mustered out after four years of continuous combat service with the artillery in Europe, and had come to the farm to think about his future. While he deliberated this problem, he made himself useful overhauling a tractor.

Now I resumed my campaign to get Margaret away on a holiday. Bud had decided to stay with us until after Christmas. Margaret, however, refused to leave unless there was a woman in the house to cook for her brother and me and to mind the children. No help was procurable in a house that had no furnace, and the plumber who had promised all summer to install one before cold weather had as yet not arrived.

"Shucks," Bud said, "there's no trick to putting in a furnace. The radiators are already here. All we have to do is set up a new boiler, hook in an oil burner, and we've got heat. Let's do it ourselves."

This we did while Margaret watched, first skeptically and then with enthusiasm. The morning came when Bud told her we would complete the job that night. Excitedly she telephoned a woman named Alice, who had agreed to cook for us if the house was warm, and then called a friend in New York to assure her that this time there would be no change in her plans. She would positively be there the next morning.

All that remained of the furnace installation was to take down from the basement ceiling a twenty-two-foot section of six-inch cast-iron pipe, the main duct from the old furnace, replace it with a short span of four-inch pipe, and light the burner. Glee and Benny came in after lunch to help take the big pipe down, for it weighed about three hundred pounds. While three of us held on firmly, Bud set a precautionary brace and began to remove the cleats that secured the pipe to the ceiling. Suddenly a strip of lath pulled loose. The brace gave way. Glee and Benny jumped. I did not. The full weight of the pipe descended on my right foot.

My boot was cut away. A local physician gave first aid and sent me thirty miles to a specialist who, after X-raying the damage, put my foot in a cast and made this pronouncement:

"The thing's so badly smashed that there's no use trying to set any bones. I've done what I can, and maybe this will knit by itself. Maybe not. At any rate, come back in a month and I'll tell you whether we have to amputate."

Margaret cried on the way home. She had no reserve of energy left with which to meet this new misfortune. Bud helped me upstairs while she telephoned to New York, once more canceling her trip. Then, surprisingly, she did not come to me.

At noon, Lampert brought me my lunch on a tray. An hour later Margaret walked past my door to her own bedroom without a word. At dinnertime, Bud waited on me. Not until bedtime did Margaret appear. She looked haggard and emotionally bankrupt.

"How are you now?" she asked listlessly.

"Okay, I guess," I said.

She tucked me up for the night, without any show of affection or sympathy.

"I telephoned to New York again," she said.

"I'm sorry," I said.

She went to the door without bidding me good night, then turned, her eyes lit with a little of their old fire.

"When you get on your feet again," she said sharply, "you'd better be careful—because I'm the one who's entitled to the next illness and I'm warning you right now I'm going to get it!"

She closed my door with a resounding slam.

CHAPTER TEN

When Margaret and I were married, I turned to her after the ceremony and said, "Now remember, I didn't promise anything except to make you happy." She must have recalled that remark, and not happily, during the year following my return from the army.

The peculiar circumstances under which I had made this statement stemmed from a good many frustrations caused by our lives in the city. Both of us had concentrated on being successful, at the sacrifice of a good many of the ingredients of a balanced life. Suddenly we had met and convinced each other of what we had really known separately all the time; namely, that there was more to life than money. Because when we were married we did not know each other too well, we set up for ourselves a standard that discounted our lack of knowledge of each other's experiences and traditions.

It accented happiness. And since I was still unsure of my ability to write lucratively enough to support a family, I reminded Margaret from time to time, though jokingly, that one day we might be compelled to change our standard of living.

"We can always fish for a living from a thirty-foot yawl," I would say. "Tie the kids on a long rope, and if they wash overboard, we can just haul them in. In fact, it might be fun."

Margaret always laughed lightheartedly, accepting the proposition that nothing much mattered except our spiritual well-being.

At the time of our marriage I was so carried away by the prospects before us that I sat up two nights writing a ceremony that had in it none of the venerable phrases of the traditional ritual. Actually, we promised each other nothing: neither to love, honor, nor cherish, certainly not to obey; for we had the feeling that these ingredients were inherent in our depth of mutuality and required no public acknowledgement. It all seemed very significant at the time, though nowadays I am inclined to remember the look of bewilderment and constrained amusement on the face of the white-haired gentleman who united us, not from words of the prayer book, but from three typewritten pages in which some last-minute changes had been made in pencil. It was legal, anyway.

We also disrupted convention in another way. The suddenness of our resolve to team our resources and go abroad had given us no time to clear the decks of those true confessions which lovers are wont to make. Thus we had a good excuse to leave the past behind, and were determined to do so.

Of course this did not work, for we could not resist the temptation to peep into these hidden rooms from time to time. For a year Margaret invented adroit devices for extracting from me little bits of history, and every time she obtained new data I could almost see it drop into a slot in her mind, in perfect juxtaposition to some tidbit she had ferreted from me earlier. She was so persistent in this that occasionally I found myself manufacturing a lotharioism rather than turning her away with a prosaic reality. During these sessions of Peeping Tom, I discovered a few things about her too. Eventually we learned all there was to know. The beauty of this process was that what we had extracted by guile must be kept secret. We could not, at tempting moments, hurl past peccadillos into each other's teeth, because we were not supposed to be aware of them.

This little game had built up in both of us a constraining reticence toward each other's individualities. Not having known Margaret's family I could not throw at her, in an argument, such a phrase as "Oh, you're as stubborn as your grandpa," or perhaps "I'd expect that of your sister but not of you." Having no background for insulting comparison, we were at a loss to dispute each other. Thus we had tended to evaluate arguments and misunderstandings from surface manifestations and settle them on the spot. Sometimes I have gagged over accepting the responsibility in a family dispute when I knew that I was not at fault, but Margaret has shown herself to be a bit more stubborn than I am, so I am more likely to bend. And I have discovered that when her inflexibility ends, as it always does, in a burst of tenderness, the misunderstanding never again arises. Margaret in turn yields more quickly than I on issues requiring decision. My snap judgments are fast, not always accurate. Ultimately in such cases, Margaret will say, "Have it your way," knowing well that, if she is right, she will eventually persuade me by woman's guile to accept her stand. Or time will prove me to have been correct, in which instance she will admit frankly that she was wrong. Always our mutual emphasis on happiness has tended, almost subconsciously, to arbitrate any differences between us.

Rather than be angry at the care which Margaret took to show me no sympathy over my broken foot, I realized that her behavior welled out of disappointment that, after the nervous strain of the war years and the exhausting restoration of the farm, she could not at last put down this burden and resume her own life.

The second afternoon of my convalescence, Lampert paid me a visit and was a splendid audience for a cripple. He asked all the proper questions, giving me serious attention through a clinical description of my seventeen fractures. I was enjoying myself, and him, when Margaret entered and led him away.

"Daddy is ill, dear," she said with an irony directed to me rather than to him, "and we'd better just leave him alone."

For food she sent up, invariably, the same fare: poached eggs on toast and a glass of milk. When the doctor called, she did not accompany him to my room, which was a hardship on her, for she never neglects an opportunity to talk to Doctor Scott whose visits to our house are more the renewal of acquaintance with an old friend than a prescription for symptoms.

On the third day of this embargo, however, I knew that she must come around. The milk had a peculiar taste. Margaret worries about our milk, since it is not pasteurized, and she constantly imagines that her children are on the verge of milk fever. Any change in the quantity or quality of the milk sets up in her an immediate reaction. Fortunately, from my rounds with the veterinarian while in the Air Corps hospital in New York State, I had learned enough to diagnose, even at this long range, the cause of the peculiar taste. One of the cows was developing mastitis, a streptococcic inflammation of the udder which, when caught in its early stages, is not likely to be serious. I did not drink my milk that noon.

Shortly thereafter, in walked Margaret. She did not ask me how I felt. Pointedly she did not look at my clumsy plaster cast, which could hardly have escaped her attention since Laurie had that morning decorated it with primitive drawings, using purple crayon. She stood just inside the door, as though I suffered from some contagion she must not breathe, and said, "I see you didn't drink your milk. Does it taste funny to you?"

"Yes," I said.

"It's never been like this before, and Glee says he doesn't notice anything odd about it. Any ideas?"

"Well—" I said, "it's hard to tell, from here."

"Bangs' Disease?"

"No, I'm sure it's not that. Undoubtedly the bacteria count is high, though, and I wouldn't let the kids drink it. It's all right for butter."

This lit some sort of torch.

"Perhaps you'd like to churn the butter," she said. "You don't seem to have anything else to do."

"Glad to," I said, "if you can get the churn up here."

"Oh, I'll do that, all right. But what about the milk?"

I guess I grinned about then, and Margaret didn't like it.

"You do know what's wrong," she said.

"Yes," I admitted.

Margaret was exasperated. "Then for goodness' sake won't you just tell me what it is and not be coy about it?"

When Margaret is that sharp she is on the verge of thawing and all that is needed to melt her is a gesture. I made it. I held out my hand and said, "Honey, come here."

She did not budge. "I'm awfully busy," she countered.

"Not too busy to hear this."

Curiosity won. Stiffly she came to the bed and I took her hand.

"A cow has mastitis," I said. "Doc Hughes can fix it in one visit."

"How do you know?" Now she was piqued that I, flat on my back, could diagnose veterinary problems better than she could. I pressed my advantage.

"I'll take care of it," I said. "If Glee comes to the house, send him up here. I'll tell him what to do."

This was legerdemain to Margaret, though it was quite simple to me. Since Glee hated to milk, he had undoubtedly turned this chore over to Benny. Hence he had not noticed the swollen udder glands which are the most obvious symptom of mastitis. Of course he would not admit to Margaret that he did not know what was going on, but he certainly would have investigated by now, and would know which cow was infected.

My willingness to move in on the farm problems, even though bedridden, was the therapeutic Margaret needed. She relaxed a little.

"And while we're about it," I said, "I want you to go to New York. Nothing can happen to me here in bed, and now that your brother has finished the furnace, we can probably get Alice. Nice and warm in here today, isn't it?"

Margaret melted.

"I'm sorry, darling," she said. "I've been mean to you."

"Not at all," I replied. "I've been mean to you. I should have been more careful with the steam pipe. It might have killed me, and then I'd never enjoy your company again."

"I'm afraid," Margaret said quickly, "that I'm not very enjoyable now." With that she left the room.

Of course she did not go to New York. But the knowledge that she might go if she so desired had a remarkable effect on her. That night she brought me a good dinner, and after the children were in bed she and Bud joined me for a game of pinochle.

As though the eye injury and the broken foot were an

augury of worse to come, the next twelve months were one trial after another. The first blow was the calf crop. We knew that Horatio, the handsome Angus bull, was not worth his two gallons of feed a day. We had kept him, however, in the hope that the calves he did sire would make up in quality what they lacked in quantity. Now his offspring began to appear. They were not imposing. A dozen were stillborn and the rest were, with a few exceptions, weak and leggy. Our first impulse, of course, was to blame Horatio for everything. In another six weeks calves of different male parentage made their appearance, and they also were weak.

This situation was not at all according to the book. The government implied quite strongly that nature had a way of taking its course on the farm. The purebred breeding association representatives went even further. They told me emphatically that the first calf would undoubtedly, at a year of age, return me the entire purchase price of the dam. All I had to do was put it on good grass after its birth. Even my inexperienced eye could see that these spindly calves would not make my fortune despite their very pretty heads. The bull calves had very high tailheads and, so far as I could see, heads identical with those of the heifers. This is not a desirable condition. Even the book says so.

What I discovered eventually was that my farm was deficient in the trace minerals. While I was feeding my cows all they could eat, their provender, grown on worn-out land, was not nutritious. The calves did not receive from their mothers enough of the minor minerals—cobalt for example—to give them a healthy start in life. The immediate remedy was to supplement the feeding of all the farm animals with an expensive mineral mixture while working out a long-range program, also expensive, of soil improvement. Thus I learned that a farm which looks beautiful to its owner is not necessarily beautiful to a cow. In all my eight hundred government bulletins, none discusses the soil from the point of view of the bovine mother. This, I feel, is an oversight.

The books on farming also say that a pair of work mares are very handy and cost nothing, because each produces a colt a year which may be sold for enough cash to pay the feed bill. In this mechanized day, work horses are too slow. You can't put a five-dollar-a-day hand to work with a team if you do cost accounting. High wages require time-saving machinery. Having made this discovery, I was reluctant to sell my mares before their revenue-attractive colts arrived, and consoled myself that at least they could plow the garden in the spring and be used to pull the corn planter. I fed them all winter. In the spring, ready to work garden and plant corn, I found the mares expecting their foals any day and therefore unavailable for farm work. One colt died at birth, the other was ruptured. Like Victorian novels, the printed romances concerning farming do not face these facts of life.

In other ways I learned that a man may not farm from a book, unless sound experience backs him up. I planted grapes, asparagus, rhubarb, and even a winter vegetable garden in cold frames, doing all these exactly according to written instructions. The grapes are a good example of this literary horticulture. They came up beautifully. When they were about six inches high, I noticed one morning that the top frond had been eaten from one of my plants during the night. The book illustrated this ailment, produced by an aphid, and recommended spraying with Bordeaux mixture. I applied the remedy carefully. Evidently this was just a condiment to the aphids, for the next day not a plant had a leaf on it and the grapes, of course, died.

108

The asparagus was a curiosity that I do not to this day understand. We set it according to instructions, in a deep trench, covering it gradually as it grew. We were tempted to cut and eat these choice young shoots, but the book said not to touch them the first year. We waited. The second year none of the asparagus came up; but by some ingenuity of nature, wild asparagus abounded in every fence row within an eighth of a mile. We did not hear about these volunteers, however, until the farm hands had harvested and consumed them. Operating then on the Louis Bromfield theory that gardeners should give plants a natural habitat and growing condition, I last year scattered asparagus seed along the fence rows where the earlier volunteer growth had appeared. This year there is no asparagus whatever along the fence rows, but there are a few volunteers in the garden, among the cabbages.

As spring came round, marking our second anniversary on the farm, I began to pay particular attention to three pure-bred heifers which had been in a feed lot all winter. They were the only prospects from my previous year's calf crop which showed those breeding qualities that are, according to the book, so easily perpetuated in the Angus breed. Because the farm needed revenue, and because I had decided the time had come to learn something about showing cattle, I entered these heifers in a show and sale.

This necessitated much special feed and handling. The animals had all to be broken to halter so they could be led, and so they would stand quietly. I treated them like so many young princesses. All winter they not only got the best grain on the farm but also expensive supplements such as linseed meal which puts on flesh evenly, grows hair, and makes the coat glisten. The heifers came along nicely except in one particular: they would not break to halter.

There are a few tricks evidently that are not in the book, or else my heifers were unusually stubborn females.

One day a representative of the forthcoming cattle show paid me an inspection visit. While we were looking at the heifers I told him of my difficulty. He suggested that two of them be sold in a pen, for which no halter-breaking was required. The most attractive of the half sisters, he said, was well worth further training.

"I hope so," I said, "because I have about two hundred and fifty dollars each in these heifers now, one way or another, and I certainly don't want to take a loss after all my work."

He assured me that, properly fitted, my little Eroica should bring double that money, so I went back to work determined that either I would break Eroica or she me. My technique was to put a halter on her and try to lead her to water or feed, then try to walk her back to the pen in which the other heifers were lodged. The book says this is a sound principle, since it gives the calf an incentive at each end of the line. Eroica, however, had other ideas and evidently responded to other incentives. She would not lead.

One warm April morning three weeks before the show I decided to school Eroica just once more. By this time she was no longer a baby, weighing close to one thousand pounds. By some reversal of temperament that is always a mystery in her sex, Eroica that morning went along with me as though she loved me. When I entered her stall she did not immediately rush into a dark corner behind her sisters, but came to me and nuzzled her cold nose in my hand. Here at last was progress. Coaxingly, caressingly, my every movement in slow motion lest I upset her, I put on her halter and lead rope and suggested a walk in the morning sun.

"Come on, baby," I crooned. "Sure, you love your old

daddy this morning, don't you? That's a good baby."

She stepped out the door with the docility of a Welsh pony and heeled me across the yard to the watering trough. While she was drinking I tied a knot in the end of the lead rope, so that if she began to play tricks on me the rope could not slip from my grasp. I scratched her ears and ran my hands along her back. She seemed to like this. The warm weather had brought out of her back those tiny parasites which in our country are called "wolves." I scratched them from her hide with a Scotch comb. Eroica rewarded me with a grateful and, I thought, coy expression of deep content. Inspired by this, I put her in a chute and with an electric razor shaved her face and poll and tail. She accepted this with the resignation of any lady in the beauty shop. With warm water and soap I washed her down and sprayed her with a fly repellent and even took a couple of practice swipes with a comb, to dress up her coat with those pretty curls the judges make so much of in the show ring. Now she did look like about five hundred dollars, and I began to feel that at last farming had its rewards. This was one of the compensations of the hard rural life, deeply gratifying.

Evidently I overdid it. For as I began to lead her back to her stall, Eroica turned up her spunky nose and refused to go. Like most ladies, she could not understand that our romance was ended, at least for today.

"Come on, baby," I coaxed her from my end of a tight lead line. "There's some nice corn waiting for you and a bale of good alfalfa. Come along, now."

I tugged on the rope.

With that she bolted. The suddenness of her thrust gave me no time to unwrap the rope from around my wrist, so for about the first ten feet she dragged me after her, while the rope burned the flesh from my hand. She broke free as I slipped in a quagmire. She raced downhill parallel to a stout plank fence. The peculiar waddling gait of a fat cow caused the lead rope to swing back and forth wildly, and finally it slipped between two planks of the fence. Eroica ran on, but the lead rope did not follow her. The knot I had tied in its end caught between a plank and a post, drawing Eroica up short. Her neck came around with a crunch of breaking bones, and she went down.

There was nothing to do except to cut her throat quickly and telephone to the butcher. We ate Eroica all summer, at a cost of approximately one dollar a pound. This is not exorbitant for tender steaks and fine linseed-fatted rolled roasts, but it takes the savor from stew meat.

Margaret was contemptuous, I knew, of my experience with the heifer, particularly since I had to call a doctor to treat my mangled hand. She did not say anything, but her implication was plain that when she had operated the farm alone she had done much better. Now, to salvage something from our heavy investment in the heifers, she took an active hand in grooming the two remaining animals for the sale.

We could not exhibit them in the morning show, since they would not lead at halter. While other exhibitors fought for blue ribbons in the show ring, Margaret was equally industrious in the barn. First she took straw and made a deep litter in the pen, so that the heifers, standing almost to their bellies in clean bedding, looked even shorter-legged than nature had endowed them. She combed out the tail ends with great care, as though preening them for Sunday School, then lightly coated the body hair with mineral oil. She brushed one heifer across the back, to conceal the fact that the topline was not absolutely straight, while on the other she slicked down the hair on one part of the belly and fluffed it up elsewhere, again to maintain the illusion of a perfectly straight line. Using a round curry comb, she made deft sweeps down the flanks of the two animals to produce a water wave, and finished her grooming by removing a few stray long hairs from the ears with a scissors. So intent was she on this undertaking that she missed the morning show, in which the prize went to a heifer almost twice as fat as either of ours, and as gentle as a spring lamb.

At lunchtime, Margaret could not join the fashionable ladies and gentlemen who sponsor purebred cattle, leaving the barn work to accomplished herdsmen, because she was covered with mineral oil, coarse black hairs, and barnlot impedimenta; but she was triumphant. Our babies did look beautiful.

The only trouble was that during the noon hour the heifers lay down in their deep bed of straw. When the time came for our lovelies to be paraded into the sales ring, they rose to their feet with bits of straw all over them, and the careful marcel gone from their sleek coats. Margaret ran beside them as they walked up the ramp, swiping them frantically with her comb and brush.

"Anyway," she told me triumphantly as the heifers went into the ring, "you'll see that showmanship pays off. What do you think they'll bring?"

I said I'd be happy to get back my two hundred and fifty dollars.

"Nonsense," Margaret snorted. "We want a profit. And looking as pretty as they do now, they'll bring it."

They brought $92.50 each. Margaret could not believe her ears when the auctioneer knocked them down at such an insulting price. She handed me the comb and brush and went outside to the truck, and there she stayed.

When I emerged from the show barn, dragging a wooden

box full of brushes, combs, mineral oil bottles, and watering pails, and loaded the truck for our return home, Margaret was still angry. She was taking this thing personally.

"I see what you mean," she said tensely, "about the purebred business."

"It has a lot of angles," I conceded, "but remember, this is our first sale. At least we have nowhere to go but up."

My cheery philosophy was ineffective.

"Up to the poorhouse," Margaret said. "We should have put these heifers in the food locker, too. We'd be money ahead."

"Well," I said, using our traditional refrain to absorb bad news, "if worst comes to worst, we can always buy a little boat and fish for a living."

"You know we can't do that," Margaret answered, this time taking me seriously.

"Why not?" I said. I was beginning to warm to the idea.

"I get seasick," she said.

CHAPTER ELEVEN

MARGARET and I are easily dis-
couraged for the moment, but we accept ultimate defeat
reluctantly. We are also stubborn in adversity, being ad-
vocates of the great American tradition that if you want
something badly enough, and go after it aggressively enough,
you'll get it.

Our humiliation over the heifers brought out our stub-
bornness. Just exactly what was wrong, we asked ourselves,
with our farming program? Nothing, we concluded, that
another fifty-thousand-dollar investment would not cure.

On a farm, there is always a necessity to spend money.
Capital investment is a chain reaction, not unlike atomic
fission, in that one expensive improvement inevitably ex-
plodes into another until finally, if you are not careful, the
whole thing blows up on you.

We had already purchased seven hundred acres and spent
half again the initial cost in improvements and repairs. In
two and a half years, income from the farm had been neg-
ligible compared with the disbursements.

Obviously, if we were to make a success of the purebred
business, we now must go out and spend again. Our chief
deficiency was a good bull. If we purchased one, this in-

vestment would result in adequate return only if we provided better facilities for the brood herd, to give them proper feed, shelter, and handling so that, at sale time, the calves would show off to best advantage the expensive bloodlines that had produced them.

So we decided to buy a new bull. Just getting a good bull is, unfortunately, not enough. In the purebred industry, it is important that the herd sire be not only handsome and virile but also expensive. Leafing through the advertisements in the *Angus Journal* we were conscious of one outstanding fact: a bull was not fashionable (and therefore not profitable) unless he had cost somebody a lot of money. One of our neighbors had about as well-bred a sire as the Angus breed boasted, yet he was not making money. He had made the mistake of purchasing this outstanding animal as a bargain at weaning time. His calves did not bring outstanding prices. Another neighbor, who had a nice enough bull which sired good though not sensational calves, sold his offerings for the price of a new automobile each. The difference was that the second bull had cost fifty thousand dollars.

The importance of this fine point was impressed on me one day when, together with a visiting authority on Angus cattle, I went to the home of my neighbor with the cheap bull. In the field we saw two score magnificent male calves about six months old. Surely, our host said, some of his animals should be raised as bulls. Certainly among them were a few the services of which would improve the breed.

The visitor agreed with the owner's estimate of their worth, but his advice was to steer the whole lot.

"If these calves were at Coiningmoney Farm (home of the fifty-thousand-dollar bull) they'd be worth money," the expert said. "On your place, without heavy advertising and impressive promotion, they aren't worth the expense of fitting them as herd sire prospects."

My friend not only steered his calves, but also sold all his purebred cows and went into the beef business. This should have been an example to Margaret and me. Instead, we kept thinking of the affluence of Coiningmoney Farm (Inc.)

"What we need," Margaret said, "is a fifty-thousand-dollar bull for about two thousand dollars."

"Find one," I said, "and we'll incorporate."

We finally found a reasonable facsimile. His name was Bando, a short form for an illustrious six word cognomen tracing him to the Bandolier family. He had won outstanding show ring prizes as a yearling and had been purchased at a price high enough to rate the newspapers. His owner then had advertised him extensively and made him fashionable.

Margaret and I became interested in Bando at a Dutchess County sale, in New York State, when J. C. Penney, one of the shrewdest buyers in the Angus business, bid one thousand dollars each for six of Bando's yearling daughters. Bando's owner was a friend of ours and we found him open to an offer. After three years of Bando's service, our friend had so many of the bull's daughters in his herd that he needed a new sire, for even in beef breeding incest is frowned on. We made a deal. I have always suspected that the fact that we were taking the mighty bull out of Dutchess County competition influenced the price in our favor. That and the fact that our friend wanted to help us to get started; many cattlemen are generous in that way.

Now the chain reaction set in. By comparison with the new bull, our cows did not look well. Princes do not, except in story books, mate with commoners, and our herd was well interspersed with Cinderellas who might, any midnight, return to the scullery. We therefore purchased a dozen fit wives for Bando, while keeping all our old cows. The herd was now so valuable that insurance on it became mandatory.

The problem of feed immediately arose, too. Our pastures, heretofore adequate for scrawny cattle, must be knee-deep in ladino clover. (Cost of the improvement, $3,500.) To insure bounteous digestible nutrients all winter, we built a silo ($1,200). Our mediocre sheds, a true reflection of our herd up to that time, were remodeled into the stately palaces required by princes of the Angus breed ($4,000). Lest one of our precious animals break a leg or lose his temper during veterinary treatments, elaborate chutes and pens were constructed ($600).

And the extra handling now required seven full-time employees, rather than three.

Unfortunately, no one has yet discovered how to market a purebred calf profitably in less time than two years after its conception. The many scientists in agriculture should study this problem seriously and do something about it, for this two years is critical. During this very expensive period the herd eats its collective head off and receives royal treatment, without bringing in a dime of revenue. Week after week the payroll for seven hands must be met, the thousands of dollars of farm expenses paid, while the bearer of this burden shuts his eyes to the staggering present and dreams of the bright future far away.

In a few months I was driven back to my typewriter to support my fat cattle. Day after day I worked on the farm, then went to my desk to write half the night. I was the slave of my large establishment, not its master. Yet always before me there was the vision of one day standing in the show ring, while a dozen offspring of the great Bando sold to J. C. Penney for one thousand dollars each, and Margaret triumphantly carried home, and mounted in a crowded walnut trophy case, another silver plate and a half-dozen blue ribbons.

To keep myself from worrying over the accumulating red ink, I developed a nocturnal imaginative routine which infallibly soothed me to sleep. It began, of course, with the birth on the farm of a bull calf so outstanding, even as he wobbled for the first time on his tottering legs, that I knew him destined for greatness. On him I bestowed my own name, Hartzell, not particularly for ego gratification but because it was a good Scottish trademark remindful that the great Angus cattle were originally Highland bred. My imagination then, happily, leaped the next eighteen months of skillful feeding and handling and merciless expense, to the moment when this calf was shown for the first time, winning his class handily at the Virginia exposition. Here there was a gratifying scene in which some millionaire offered, and was refused, ten thousand dollars for my champion. The next scene, a year later, took me and the bull to the Iowa State Fair, for being originally an Iowan, I must display my success before the friends of my youth. The great Hartzell, now reaching the fullness of his powers, won easily. Six months later, when Hartzell was a three-year-old, I took him to the show of all shows, the International in Chicago, along with five yearlings sired by him (all of them, of course, sensational!) and led him out at last to be crowned international champion, his calves having won the blue ribbon for get of sire. Again the millionaire approached, this time with one hundred thousand dollars in his hand, and I gave him the classic reply of a breeder for whom this dream did once come true: "I wouldn't know what to do with a hundred thousand dollars, pardner, but I shore know what to do with a good bull."

Significantly, this wish-fulfilling vision always skipped over two important details. First, the cost of preparing a bull for outstanding competition, and second, the know-how necessary to bring even a naturally superior animal to the evenness of finish, the benignity of manner, the high style, that influence cattle judges.

One night, perhaps in summer just after a cold bath, I saw for the first time the ridiculousness of my dream. I would never get to the International, or the Iowa State Fair, or even the Eastern Regional, with any calf. I simply did not possess the skill or—equally important—the money. With the money, I might hire the know-how; possessing the skill, I might borrow the money. Possessed of neither, my calves, regardless of their parenthood, were very likely to stand where they had stood in my one show experience —at the bottom.

Chilled by this reality, I went out the next morning to look at my herd. Bando's first children were about three months old. They were short-legged, deep, with plenty of spring in the ribs and handsome heads. The bull calves looked virile even at that age, and the heifers, so alike that with difficulty I could tell them apart, were real ladies. I had the peculiar sensation that I was on another farm, looking at someone else's herd, so great was the improvement over the previous year. Even calves by indifferent cows had a certain style.

But at what cost! A year's payroll for seven men, hay and grain cultivated on three hundred acres, another three hundred acres of well-fenced, well-drained, well-improved pasture, staggering expenditures for repair and maintenance, machinery, and buildings. Gasoline for the tractors was a six-hundred-dollar item alone. Offsetting this colossal budget was a pretty herd of fat cattle, a set of uniformly excellent calves, and some well-manured fields.

My eye caught and held three heifers which were grazing along a fence row. They were holdovers from the previous year, and therefore the daughters of ill-fated Horatio. I had kept them originally because they were the best-conformed of the crop and might be worth adding to the herd. With the arrival of Bando they did not seem worthy of him, and I had been fattening them for beef. Now I had an idea.

How much had I learned about fattening cattle in these bitter two years? Had I gained sufficient know-how to go on into a profitable enterprise, or should I confess defeat? The time had come to find out.

I walked to the calf barn, opened the door, and drove the heifers into it. A sale of purebred cattle was to be held nearby three months hence. These cattle would be my entries. They were already agreeably fat, and should respond to forced feeding. I did not expect too much—merely some sign, some token that would prove to me what I must know.

In the next few weeks I attended several cattle auctions, running up in my mind a comparison between these offerings and my own. By sale date I had decided that, at the present market, my calves must bring three hundred and fifty dollars each. If they did that, I would stay in business.

They didn't quite make it. The poorest one, in my opinion, did crack three hundred. The other two sold twenty-five dollars under their half sister. But, as a friend of mine quickly pointed out, this was an improvement over my first venture in auction selling and these heifers definitely were not daughters of the well-publicized bull. I had not been at the bottom of the sale this time—just two-thirds of the way down. I had improved.

Margaret had not attended the sale. Although never before superstitious, she had feared that she might bring me bad luck. She was on the porch when I arrived at home in my empty cattle truck. She walked out to the road.

"Well," she said gaily, "at least you didn't bring them back home."

"No, they're gone," I said.

"Are we still in business?"

This, of course, was the important question. Somehow, sitting up high in a truck cab looking down at an anxious wife, I did not feel like making a decision. Behind Margaret, as she faced me, was the backdrop of the great house on which she had spent hundreds of laborious hours, many of them on hands and knees. Just over her left shoulder were the living room windows, and through my mind went the entire metamorphosis of that room. Her tears over the four layers of unremovable wallpaper. Her excitement when the oak floors shed the grime of years and emerged mellow and golden. The triumphant day when she had bought at an auction a gold-leaf mirror that fitted exactly the space above the fireplace. The jubilant evening when she found, in an old book, the design for the cabinet that might be built into a doorframe between the living room and the library. The epic occasion when the Chinese rug arrived and was put down, softening with its reds and pinks and beiges the too-bright white marble mantel. And the day we returned from a two-week lecture tour in midwinter to find the house so damp that the new living room draperies had shrunk nearly fourteen inches and were, of course, hopelessly short. And well I remembered the day Glee and I had rearranged that room's furniture eight times while Margaret sat in the doorway squinting through three-quarter closed eyes, and then the next day rearranged it just once more.

No, this was too grave a question to be settled on the high cab of a cattle truck. More was involved here than success or failure at farming. Margaret's face was strained, her large brown eyes ready to become frightened as she awaited my reply.

"I don't know any more than when I left," I said. "As an experiment, it didn't prove much, one way or the other."

Margaret was content with that. With her, vacillation is infinitely more satisfactory than decision, for it maintains the status quo. No woman likes to face the prospect of uprooting her home, even one that has caused her endless agony.

Dinner, long delayed, was on the table when I entered the house. I knew from the smell of it that Margaret had expected the worst, for she set before me all my favorite dishes. One of my few gratifications with farming was the bounteous table it afforded. Here, discreetly, was a reminder of that opulence of provender which only the farmer and the very wealthy man can afford: a twelve-pound rib roast of prime beef, creamed turnips, a garden-crisp lettuce and carrot salad, hot corn muffins with rhubarb marmalade, a big pitcher of whole milk, a slab of fresh-turned butter. Even if Laurie had not immediately blurted the secret she had been admonished to keep, I should have known there was a pie in the oven for dessert. Margaret's wild raspberry pie is a work of art, usually reserved to soften me up for the news that she has again overdrawn her checking account.

Now, like a Thanksgiving dinner, this culinary richness was spread out to ease the blow of my inadequacy as a farmer. The children hung up my coat and escorted me to my chair. The carving knife was sharp, for a change. In the face of such a demonstration, who could concede to failure?

By the time the pie appeared I had resolved that there must be a way to keep all this, if I could just find it.

CHAPTER TWELVE

WE clung like mountain goats to a precarious slope all that fourth summer of our country life. The herd of one hundred cows grazed romantically across a gentle slope, with the panorama of the Blue Ridge Mountains as a backdrop. Calves leaped about, playing kittenishly in groups along the shady fence rows. The noble bull Bando, his work as sire completed for the season, aloofly eyed his great family. Visitors commented on the idyl they witnessed from our front porch, and particularly on how fortunate we were to be the owners of all this munificence and contentment.

What these guests did not see was the preparation to feed and bed the herd during the coming winter. Cattle eat prodigiously. Two hundred tons of good hay, baled and neatly stacked in a big barn, appear to compose a mountainous pile sufficient to feed the entire county. This view is particularly in focus after several days of backbreaking labor salvaging that hay from the field. First there is the consideration of whether the hay is right to cut; then whether the weather is agreeable, since rain might ruin it. Under the impetus of a benign weather forecast, the mower is attached to the tractor, a job for a truly skilled mechanic. The hay is mowed. Anxious eyes now scan the sky as the

sun cures the new hay. Numerous trips are made to the field, where a handful of the cut grass is picked up and crumpled to be sure it is "curing right," although what could be done if it were not, short of an electric hay drier, has never been discovered. Next morning, after a night of imagining that one hears rain on the roof, the side delivery rake is hitched to the tractor and the hay is windrowed. This job is not difficult, if one keeps in mind that the rows, when completed, must lie in such a way that the baler later can run down them without lost motion. Intent on this problem, one is apt to forget that the rake, being an eccentric device built on a bias, will also swing on a bias if given its own way. Turning a side delivery rake in a field, hard by a fence row overgrown to a dense mat of honeysuckle, is a tricky maneuver.

Benny, for the first time manipulating the rake, attempted despite careful warnings to swing about at the end of a row without slackening speed. He learned the folly of his heedlessness when the rake swung with such force that the tractor bucked over on two wheels, throwing Benny from his seat directly into the revolving fingers of the rake. Before the tractor came to a stop against a fence post, Benny had been wrapped like a mummy in a ball of honeysuckle vines and deposited face downward in a nest of wild quail eggs. We had to cut him free with a machete. To this day Benny will not rake hay with what he calls the "tarnation machine."

A few hours of sun dry out the hay in the windrow. By this time, usually, the weather forecast augurs rain. Cut hay will survive a shower, but windrowed grass will not. A tension creeps over the farm now. No matter if the dairy cows go unmilked and the purebred calves unfed, the hay must be brought to the barn. Consultations are held in the field every five minutes. Bare arms are thrust deeply into the windrow, to feel the heat and moisture. Hay baled damp is liable to spontaneous combustion, and many a barn has burned because the hay was harvested green. Finally, as black clouds begin to make up over the mountains, the hay takes on the proper crackle, and a ball of it, held tightly in the hand, jumps up when the fingers are opened. The pickup baler is cranked and is away down the snaky line of windrow, a tractor wagon following behind to load the one-hundred-pound bales. A rhythm develops as the baler spews out its bundles and the following crew heaves them to the wagon with a motion that spares the muscles of the back. The dark clouds move closer. Now the baler breaks down. The tension of the binder twine must be adjusted to almost every cutting of hay, depending on the moisture content—again a job for an expert. Ten minutes of frantic tinkering follow, during which the wagon crew debates whether to make for the barn with half a load or wait. They always decide to wait. The baler starts again. The bales pile up. Where a moment ago was a ragged windrow there is now cleanly cropped grass, punctuated at neat intervals by a heavy bale. The baler gets ahead. After loading the wagon twice, and un-loading its contents in the barn, the crew begins to feel the weight of the hay. Each bale seems to be full of sash weights. Calls for the water boy become more frequent. No man will admit that his back aches beyond relief, or confess the dis-comfort of his itching skin where perspiration has caked on him a layer of dust and hay seeds. All day this goes on, until those who most anxiously worried over the black clouds on the horizon now pray for some canopy to blot out the cruel sun.

Once I invited a city lawyer to the hayfield, suggesting that he might be interested in observing the mechanization

that had come to the farm. From the comfort of a wagon he watched the baler at work, and finally allowed that anyone could sit on a tractor and run that thing. I put him on the tractor. He did not make one round of the field. In the shade of the first white oak tree he crept down from the seat, exhausted by the burning sun, choked by the swarming dust, bruised by the rough ride. He thought, however, that he might drive the truck while two stalwarts loaded bales. This did not last long, either. A truck is an infernal machine, requiring strong muscles, especially when it must be stopped constantly on sloping hillsides, its brakes holding not only its own weight but that of a heavy wagon hitched behind. The constant stopping and starting again exhausted my friend. He climbed shaking from the truck cab, staggered to the shade of a fence row, drank all our water, and disappeared. He ate salt pills the rest of the day. Every city man, intent on becoming a farmer, should spend one full day in the hayfield as a prerequisite to purchasing his Idylmere.

I do not know why skillful management cannot alleviate a simple complexity of farming that occurs at grain harvest, but seemingly it cannot do so. Invariably the combine, which has been tuned, inspected, and greased the day before the oats cutting, will not work when the crew is assembled. Harvesting requires many hands. In addition to the combine operator there is a man aboard to tie the sacks as they fill with grain and, having piled five or six on a platform, to trip a pedal which drops them onto the field. Three men are then required to follow along and pick up the grain, take it to the barn, pour it into the bins, and bring the empty sacks back to the field, for no farmer ever has enough sacks to do the whole job. Sacks, like ice cream, melt away.

Get five men together at one time, in itself an accomplishment in these days of acute shortages of farm labor, and the combine will not start. Either the engine refuses to fire (it is a tricky two-cylinder job operating from a magneto), or it is discovered that rats have, during the night, eaten great holes in the canvas treadle that pulls the cut grain stems into the threshing mechanism, or four vital bolts have miraculously come loose and there are no replacements available short of a hardware store eight miles away. I have yet to see a combine crew, budgeted to start work at ten in the morning and finish a field by five in the afternoon, get under way before half-past eleven, which of course is just a half hour before dinner. The labor loss in waiting time soon mounts up. In addition, the combining is finished so late in the day that the crew must be bribed into working two hours overtime, then wheedled into doing the ordinary farm chores after dark. Skill is required in combining, too. If the mechanism is not properly set, most of the grain either will remain on the chaff or fall to the ground. Stamina is the greatest requisite. A sack containing two bushels of wheat weighs one hundred and ten pounds. The man who has lifted three hundred sacks from the ground in one day, loaded them on a wagon, and unloaded them from the wagon into a bin, knows from his aching back that he has done a job that day. It is not a chore for the city man to attempt lightly, requiring as it does much muscle building. Lifting trucks from mudholes and cleaning manure from a feed lot with thirty-five pounds of manure on each forkload, are considered the proper training for hoisting sacks of grain. Carrying home a few groceries from the corner delicatessen is not quite enough muscle building for farm requirements.

Putting corn into a crib is another task to ponder long upon before attempting. In these days, the more affluent farmers have mechanical elevators for this chore, but they are such a luxury that a man starting in agriculture will not possess one. Corn is generally picked by a mechanical picker in the fields, the shucked ears falling into a wagon. Unfortunately these wagons must be unloaded into the crib, and here is a real ordeal. The first load is easy. The unloader, manipulating a scoop shovel, throws the corn *down* from the wagon onto the crib floor. As the crib fills, the operator must throw the corn *up*, and as the day wears on, and his muscles wear out, he must throw his loaded shovel ever higher and higher. A scoop of corn weighs about twelve pounds, more or less. By nightfall, after a day of this labor, the empty scoop seems to weigh about fifty pounds and even a level scoopful about one hundred.

Two years ago a diligent young hand named Brewster, who was afraid of losing an arm on the mechanical picker, and who had tried to level the corn in the wagon only to be hit several times on the head by corn belching from the hopper, elected the job of unloading the wagons into the crib. Usually we spell this work, and we were delighted to have a volunteer. Brewster worked nobly all day. He shoveled about one hundred barrels (a barrel, or "barl" as it is called here, is five bushels) of corn without complaint. The next day he did not show up for work, although our corn was still only one-third harvested. We sent a boy to Brewster's house to fetch him, but Brewster declined to appear.

"All night long I shoveled that cawn," was the message he sent back, "and the cawn gittin' higher an' higher till I gits so dizzy I doan' rest a wink. Today, I sleep."

Farm work can be so exhausting that sleep is impossible afterwards. When we were installing a new pump at the barn, Benny's job was to stand at the pipe threader, which works by hand, and thread pipe all day long. Threading a four-inch, or even a three-inch pipe on a hand threader is a physically exhausting job. Benny, usually cheerful, grew more and more taciturn as the day advanced, his good nature returning only when a half-inch or inch pipe came along to give him respite. We completed the job in one day, and luckily, for the next morning Benny was mournful.

"What's the matter, Benny?" I asked, for it is important to humor field hands and cajole them out of their troubles.

Benny half opened his eyes, and shook his head.

"Threaded pipe all night," he groaned. "But could I get any half-inch pipe to rest up on? No, suh. Nothin' but threes and fours."

Had the farm been making money, and had I been able to visualize an agreeable cash return for the backbreaking labor of that summer, I should perhaps have been philosophical. Instead, all that arduous season I felt a growing feeling of resentment that I worked so hard for nothing. At least Glee, Benny, Brewster, and the other hands were being paid cash by the hour, plus a good house, firewood, milk, meat, cornmeal, and flour, for their hire. They knew what they were doing. I, on the other hand, was getting no return except ague, shooting pains, aching back, calluses, sunburn, and grease-packed cuts and contusions, plus, of course, a staggering assortment of bills payable.

Resentment welled up in me, then self-pity, then indignation, until by September, during the lespedeza harvest, I crept toward the house after a hard day of haying, convinced at last that I was the greatest sucker of all time. I supported one hundred cows, one hundred calves, thirty steers, an elegant bull and one not so elegant, three milch cows, two horses, fifty hogs, seven families (not counting my own) and sundry guineas and chickens (not to mention quail, rabbits, foxes, birds, rats, and my neighbor's flock of geese) in the greatest of luxury, while I, the alleged beneficiary, derived less from my effort than the field hands.

My mood was further aggravated by another peculiar characteristic of farming that I have not been able to understand. For some weeks the hog market had been hovering at around thirty dollars a hundred pounds. I had sent twenty-four fat hogs to town that morning. By some unaccountable but infallible legerdemain, the market that day was what is known as "away off" and my hogs, although near the day's top, had brought only $25.40. It is axiomatic that the market drops on the day you ship choice stock. The only time you hit a rising market is when you've sent only an old worn-out dairy cow that is just stew meat anyway.

Walking across the field, I recalled the experience of an Iowa farmer who, during the depression years, had shipped a lot of good steers to Chicago. For all his initial investment, his year of feeding, his labor of getting in the crops those cattle had consumed, he had realized less than nothing. Instead of getting a check from his Chicago dealer, he received an itemization of the freight, handling, and commission charges, and a bill for $17.10, expenses which his good steers had not quite covered.

If I, I thought, cannot make a go of this thing when farm prices are the highest in history, what will I do when things are not so favorable? Everything now is in my favor. Everything, that is, except the one outstanding necessity: knowledge. What little I had learned in three years had taught me, actually, only one thing: that without years of practice, intensive knowledge, strenuous frugality, and instinctive trading ability, nobody but a chucklehead would try farming. I was a chucklehead indeed. And oh, my aching back!

In the clarity of this vision, something else became obvious that had been happening before my eyes but to which previously I had attached no significance. My family was just marking time.

The main hall, which was to have been redecorated that summer, was untouched. The flower garden that was to have been started was not even on paper. The sandpile for the children was unconstructed. Even the vegetable garden, in former years rich with provender, was unfruitful and unattended, and there had been no bustle in the kitchen such as accompanies the canning and deep-freezing activities of the womenfolk. Obviously, none of my household expected us to remain at Gaston Hall. Nothing had been put by to feed us during the winter. Margaret had not attended an auction sale, searching for furniture bargains, for some months. She had not encouraged callers, or given parties. No replacement had been secured for the departed cook. My family was standing by, like an army awaiting marching orders.

Weary as I was, I trudged upstairs, stood a long time under a shower, shaved, and came down looking respectable. For some weeks I had fallen into the slovenly habit of appearing for dinner in my work clothes, too weary to change. Margaret noticed the difference. She was in the living room —the only room in the house that was completely renovated —supervising the children's playing of phonograph records. A game of solitaire, an increasingly absorbing habit of hers that summer, was spread out before her. She looked up as I came in and, over the background of "Farmer in the Dell" said: "Things must be looking up."

"Definitely," I replied.

"Want to talk?"

This is Margaret's way of backing into a conversation until she can see a clear path through the verbiage.

"Yes," I said. "Let's go out on the porch."

She stacked a half-dozen records on the record-changer, to keep the children interested, ran to the kitchen to turn off the gas under her dinner, took off her apron, and joined me. The mountains that night were a particularly deep blue. Two years ago I should have exclaimed over the coloring. Now I thought: deep blue, no rain tomorrow, we can get in the rest of the hay.

The cattle were head down, grazing across the gently rising slope of pasture before us. Over their heads coursed forty miles of verdant valley, the greenery broken by the white sheeting of Logan Golsan's barn and the gleaming pillar of Doctor Yaeger's concrete silo. The sun, angling downward, splotched great streaks of pink and crimson ruffles over the cloud cap of the mountains. Every day for two years I had seen these mountains, in gloom and fog and mist and snow and clear blue beauty, and always they had been just a barometer to me. Now, welling out of my boyhood in the parsonage, came an old, familiar quotation from the Scripture. "I will lift up mine eyes unto the hills."

Margaret had seated herself on a bench. She was waiting, and she knew what she waited for. I kept looking at the mountains, while the rest of the song of David went through my mind. It settled me, somehow.

"I think," I said, turning then to Margaret, "that the time has come to start fishing from a thirty-foot yawl. I'm not getting anywhere, and we might as well face it and get it over with."

"All right," Margaret replied quietly, as though her answer had been ready a long time. "Our happiness is the important thing, and you are not happy. The place certainly should sell now at a profit—after all we've done to it. And—" she smiled wanly, "you said when we bought it that it was just an investment we could turn over."

"That's right, I did," I said. I had not recalled that aspect of the purchase for a long time.

"If we must sell," Margaret went on, her voice rising as it does when she is under strain, "do it quickly. I can't bear to live here much longer, knowing I'm going to move."

"I know," I said. The farm life and the community had taken hold of us; there was no doubt about that. When we had time to think about it we knew that, with a little more leisure and a little less strain, what the land had done for our Argentine friend was actually just waiting to influence us. But we seemed to be fighting the intrusion of those very qualities that we had originally sought in the country. We would not let the sun in upon our gloom. Happiness was just over the Blue Ridge somewhere; but like the fog that in October crept down, a white caterpillar, out of the hills and ambled gently across the valley, it always stopped just short of our own gate.

"I'll list the place with the real estate people tomorrow," I said.

Dinner that night was a silent repast. Even the children, usually talkative and gay, were quiet. That both of them were worn out from a day in the hayfield, carrying the water bucket, did not occur to me. Deep in my own thoughts, I attributed their taciturnity to my own despair.

Many persons came to look at the farm.

Margaret was generous in escorting these prospects about the property, and I felt very proud of her until, one day, I happened to be within earshot and discovered that, as usual with any industry on her part, there was guileful motive.

This particular pair of prospects, a man and a woman, under escort of a bantam real estate agent from a neighboring city, were obviously moneyed folk. They had read a

few books on the gratifications of rural living and were eager to build their own country romance. I arrived as the man was saying to Margaret, "What I have in mind is a place where I won't have to do any work. Just turn out a bunch of steers and let them multiply."

Margaret tried unsuccessfully to hide a smile, but she made no effort to acquaint him with any of the facts of husbandry, for city men do not like to be disillusioned about farming, as a rule, until they have spent a lot of money and time enjoying their agricultural ignorance.

Instead, with great care, Margaret pointed out to the couple that the swimming pool had no bottom, the tennis court no backstop wire, and that the basement of the house was shored up, in spots, by steel jacks to keep the joists from collapsing. She mentioned that some of our calves had died of trace mineral deficiency, and that we had cut the merchantable timber. She even pointed out that one of the tractors, which had been offered along with the land, was held together by baling wire. Within a very few minutes the inspection ended. Gaston Hall remained with us.

"What did you have to say all those things for?" I up-braided her. "There are a million things wrong with every farm, but you don't have to call attention to them. Emphasize what's good—there's plenty of that."

Margaret was all innocence.

"You don't want me to be dishonest, do you?" she inquired.

"No, but you might admire the new silo, and not go sticking knives into the beams under the big barn. The way you demonstrated how many timbers need replacing would scare off anybody."

"I think they ought to know what faces them. If we had known . . ."

"We'd never have bought this farm in the first place," I interrupted, completing her sentence. "And nobody will take it off our hands, either."

The next prospect I conducted about the farm myself. In spite of all the work we had done, I had to answer a lot of questions. Margaret eavesdropped on us along toward the end. She seemed to enjoy my discomfort at confessing that the foundation in the dairy barn was about gone, and that the estimate I had from a contractor to repair my principal tenant house was around seven thousand five hundred dollars.

She undertook to help me out.

"The swimming pool can be repaired very easily," she said brightly.

"We don't swim," the man said. He was a beagle sort of fellow, with a restless nose and darting eyes, and he was accompanied by a largish wife in a new mink coat. He was a used-car salesman, he said.

"And I hope you saw the tennis court," Margaret went on.

"We don't play, and we have no children," the woman replied. "My husband has worked hard all his life, and now that he's retiring he needs a place where he can keep from being idle."

"That's a farm, all right," I said with some feeling.

But not our farm.

The next inspection almost made me ill. A blustery man, his fingernails bitten to the quick on both hands, drove up alone in a robin's-egg-blue Cadillac. Even before he summoned me I had taken a dislike to him. He walked up the steps with an air at once condescending and proprietary, scrutinized our silver door knocker for a moment, then knocked and stood back. His face was a blank when I

144

opened the door. Here, I thought, is a horse trader, a big operator, a man who can make a dictaphone hum.

"Understand this place is for sale," he said.

"That's right."

"It's certainly big enough."

"We like a lot of room."

"But you can't keep it, huh?"

I shrugged that one off.

"Inefficiency has ruined farming in this country," he went on. "Inefficiency and stupidity. There's no reason why a farm can't be run like any other business. You're in the red here, of course?"

"Oh, yes."

"Knew it the moment I laid eyes on you."

"If you'd like to look around—" I began, but he held up his hand.

"Don't rush me," he said. "Just be quiet."

With that he stepped into the house. We are particularly proud of the hall, which extends entirely through the house from the large front porch to a spacious porch at the rear.

"Not much here," the man said. He walked into the living room, turned about immediately and came out again.

"Too small," he said. "Architecture of all these old houses is bad. They built great big houses with dinky little rooms."

"They had no central heating then, you know," I intervened. "The room size was limited by the heating capacity of the fireplace."

"Fireplace in every room, I suppose."

"Oh yes, with marble mantels."

"Inefficient heat," he said. "Show me the second floor."

Here the plumbing was inefficient. He returned to the hall.

"Have to rip the whole inside out of this house," he said.

"Start over. From the floors up. Big living room. You can get it by ripping out that fireplace in the hall, where there's too much waste space. Panel the library in walnut veneers and put in indirect lighting. Cut those boxwood down outside, too; library's too dark. Take those didos down off all the ceilings—too ornate for modern living. And those big wings—colossal waste. How many Btu's are required to heat one wing one day at zero temperature?"

"It hardly ever gets to zero around here."

"I knew you didn't know," he said. "Need a new heating plant."

"The one we have is only two years old."

"Steam," he scoffed. "Forced air, that's the economical heat. I see you're weather-stripped. How about rock wool?"

"These walls are four brick thick. There's no place to put any other insulation."

"Fantastic," he replied. "Well, how much you asking for the place?"

"You don't want to see the farm?"

"You said it was losing money; that's all I need to know. Have to start from scratch there, too, just like in the house."

He retired to the front porch, not even noticing the mountains. "What price did you say?"

"I didn't say."

"You're selling, aren't you? That's what they told me in Charlottesville."

"Who's your dealer?"

"I don't mess with dealers. Why should I pay some punk five per cent for doing what I can do myself? Knock off the agent's commission and quote me the price."

"Are you seriously interested?"

"I never ask for a price until I'm ready to buy."

"You're ready, then."

146

"If the price is right."

"But you haven't seen the farm. How can you tell whether any price is right?"

"This farm is a hollow shell. You know it and I know it. What is it you have here, seven hundred acres?"

"Seven hundred and eighteen."

"At fifty dollars an acre that's thirty-five—well, say forty thousand dollars and give you a break. Take it or leave it."

"No, thank you."

"You think it's worth more?"

"Unquestionably."

"You Virginians put too high a value on antiquity," he said, descending the porch steps. "That's why you're all failures."

With that he drove away.

I walked back into the house. My eyes swallowed up its beautiful architectural details, its gracious rooms, its bold, handsome woodwork. I tried to imagine how the house would look with the hall and living room thrown together, lighted by indirect fluorescent fixtures, no doubt; and the library, paneled in veneers. No image would come at all. The thing was unimaginable. I was angry. And I knew, also, that I could not sell the place. It had become too much a part of me. Tear it inside out, indeed!

That evening, having our coffee on the porch, I described to Margaret my encounter that afternoon. She did not comment, but she was indignant, as though someone had criticized one of the children.

"We can't go away and leave this behind," I said at last.

Margaret smiled quickly, her eyes on the mountains.

"I hoped you would say that."

"There must be some other way."

"I hope so," she said, and went to put the children to bed.

The mountains were hazy, heralding rain. A fingerling fleece tail of cloud lay horizontally across the orange ball of sun. Below the cloud the sky was very blue, and above moss green crowned with fire. The broad valley, green despite a drought, pushed down out of the mountain and moved gently upland toward me across the meadows to the boxwood bushes at my feet. All this was mine. Not the seven hundred acres of farm, the hundred cows, the fifty pigs; they lay over the hills to right and left, out of sight, at that moment detached and far away. The mountain ridge, the sunset that now mounted like a forest fire above the hills, the tall gracious house which faced this panorama, these were mine.

I did not really care about the farm. The pride of ownership had been sweated out of me. This house and what it meant to us, this valley that sheltered goodly people some of whom were now becoming our friends, meant something surely. Throw the farm away, if need be, but keep the house, the valley, and the view.

My thinking thus straightened out, I began to get an idea. I did not know how it might develop, but it was there. When Margaret rejoined me I did not speak of it. We sat a long time in silence, until only the profile of the mountains was discernible far away.

CHAPTER THIRTEEN

W HEN we had bought Gaston Hall, the auctioneer had put up the place under two different proposals. The first was to sell the farm as a single unit. The other was to divide the property into four tracts which were auctioned separately. If the bids for the four tracts totaled more than the high offer for the farm as a unit, the property would be broken up. This is a common custom among auctioneers disposing of a large property. Often an attractive small acreage, well located for subdivision, is worth more than the entire remainder.

After I had bid in the tract as a whole, the auctioneer had offered, in separate lots, the four parcels designed to attract special buyers. One was a one-hundred-and-fifty-acre piece bounded by a back road at the extreme south of the farm. Another was sixty acres well suited to subdivision on a cluster of hills abutting the surfaced road near the town of Somerset. The house and one hundred and sixty acres was included in a third lot, and the rest of the farm, comprising the chief farm buildings and four hundred and eighteen acres of good crop land, was the final offering.

I remembered that there had been a good bid for the back one hundred and fifty, from a prosperous dairyman who lived adjacent to it. There had been two bids on the potential subdivision: one from a promoter who wished to build there some cheap houses, the other from a landowner who did not want a shantytown between his porch and the mountains. There had been no interest in the other two parcels.

I had an idea that the threat of subdivision still worried my western neighbor, particularly since the farm was again for sale; and that the dairyman, encouraged by the current high price of raw milk, might still be interested in the south tract. Why not, therefore, since all that Margaret and I wanted was the house, a small acreage, and the mountain view, go back to the auctioneer's original plans and sell off three pieces of our big farm? We would then have left all we could handle, a tract big enough to operate a simple and possibly profitable beef-fattening program, and we would be compelled, by reduced land and facilities, to liquidate our costly purebred cattle. There was an added attraction here, too. We had bought the farm just before an inflation in land values. What I proposed to sell might very nearly yield us enough to secure Gaston Hall and a modest farm for practically nothing.

This sounded very good when I thought about it. Bringing it to fruition was another matter. Any inkling that such a project was in my mind would immediately depress the price.

I sent out a feeler first to the neighbor who had been anxious concerning the subdivision. People often will pay more to protect what they have than to increase their holdings. I reasoned that if I owned my neighbor's place, I would secure that sixty acres rather than have before me the perpetual threat of an unsightly foreground. The fact that my neighbor did not have enough crop land, and this sixty acres was all tillable, seemed to me to enhance the proposal considerably.

My neighbor was quick to see these advantages, too, and closed the deal promptly, fearful perhaps that I might change my mind or the entire farm might be sold. The price was substantial but not unreasonable. It was, in fact, exactly the amount offered two days later by the erstwhile promoter, who was miffed that I had not given him equal opportunity to make an offer. He undoubtedly would have gone a little higher.

Flushed with this success, I retired part of my mortgage and began to stalk the dairyman. Here was an entirely different problem. The dairyman is prosperous because, in addition to being an excellent farmer, he is also a shrewd trader. When he buys anything, he gets full value for his money. The land I offered him was not as valuable as the tract already sold, since it was on the back road and in part comprised cut-over timber. Again I emphasized the urgency of my proposition. If the entire farm was sold, the dairyman perhaps never again in his lifetime would have opportunity to secure this land that joined his own fences.

For several weeks we negotiated cautiously. Obvious at the outset was one fact. The dairyman knew exactly how much money per acre that land was worth to him in terms of milk production, and that was all he was going to pay. He was going to get it for less if possible. The game was for him to discover how much less I would take, and for me to guess, from our conversations, how much milk he thought that land would produce. In all this we did not once mention price. Like two chess players at the beginning of a game, we waited for the other fellow to make a mistake. We rode over the land on horseback several times and walked the proposed fence line. We mutually weighed each word cautiously before we spoke. All the time I was asking myself, "If I were a dairyman, what would that land be worth to me?" Finally I did what should have been obvious earlier. I called in a good dairyman and asked him the same question. He gave me an opinion that was exactly the amount I had already speculated my prospective purchaser might, if pressed, agree to. This was progress. It did not occur to me that my neighbor might have put this price into my consultant's head. In retrospect, however, I am inclined to believe that he may have. As I said, he is a clever fellow, and he was at that time a county Triple-A committee colleague of my consultant.

Now the dairyman and I got down to details—except price. What about the cost of fencing the new boundary? Who would pay for the survey and for writing the deed? The legal expense? The transfer tax stamps? Should a gate be set into the fence so that we could borrow equipment back and forth? If so, should the gate be kept padlocked? The most minute questions were mulled and decided, the riparian rights searched, modified, and bargained for. Still no mention of price. By now the dairyman knew that I had made up my mind, I knew that he had made up his, and each of us appreciated that the other would not budge, once the declaration was made. He wanted to buy, I to sell; yet if, as was probable, there was a difference of opinion on that vital matter of price per acre, we would be deadlocked, and neither of us would give; he because he could not justify it in terms of production; I because sale of that land would depreciate the value of the remainder of the farm. Cognizant each of the other's problem, we stalled.

This caution disrupted the bargaining. Neither of us would make the first offer, for the first to talk money is implied to be the more anxious. Neither of us would be put in the position of urgency.

Finally every conceivable question had been explored,

every possible answer given, and there was nothing else to talk about except price and the weather. We talked weather for several meetings and then, for lack of conversation, we began to avoid each other. If I saw the dairyman coming into the crossroads store, I ducked out the back door. If we met in the post office, he hurried away to deliver his milk to the railroad station. Two months passed, and spring planting was almost upon us, before this impasse was broken.

I broke it. Spring is the great season for rural sales. City folk yearn to become farmers most intensely when forsythia is in bloom. A man came along who wanted to buy Gaston Hall. He was serious about it, and his offer was attractive. Either the dairyman and I came to terms, or we moved. There was no alternative.

I went to the dairyman and told him exactly what I wanted to do: keep part of the farm and sell the remainder. My honesty was obvious. Therefore he could not doubt my honesty when I went on to say that I had, at that moment, a buyer for the entire farm. If he wanted the back tract, it was now or never.

"How much do I have to pay for it?" he asked. With him, too, the time for caution had gone by.

I mentioned a price. Quickly he told me what he thought the acreage was worth. We were only five dollars an acre apart. We split the difference. Thus there was victory all around. He had been pressed a little beyond his calculations; I had been squeezed a little below my rock bottom. We were both happy.

Now all that remained was to dispose of the four hundred acres and the bulk of the farm buildings. Here again, was a problem. This tract had no outlet except over my entrance road, necessitating an expensive job of road building. The main house, while a fine colonial structure of nine rooms, had no electricity, only token plumbing, and was generally dilapidated. What it needed was a seventy-five-hundred-dollar renovation.

For some peculiar reason (the same was true of us) potential farmers judge an agricultural property more by the house than by the land. A farm containing a beautiful house on worn-out land will sell attractively. Magnificent land attended by a shabby dwelling has little value. Margaret and I took part of the dairyman's money and with it restored the colonial house. Then we put the tract up for sale, through agents.

No buyer was interested. The lack of an entrance road was a block none could penetrate. Most of the prospects remarked that, since they had to spend considerable money on farm machinery, they did not want the added immediate expense of roadbuilding. When obviously the acreage was not going to sell, I took another hard look at the possibility of farming five hundred acres rather than one hundred and sixty. By now I had become so enthusiastic over the prospect of liquidating my expensive purebred herd, and being rid at last of the attendant losses and responsibilities and labor, that I had been putting in order as a steer-fattening farm the parcel that would remain to Gaston Hall. It became evident that I should not need most of my costly equipment when the farm was to be composed entirely of pastureland and hayfields.

I offered my farm machinery as an added inducement with the tract that was for sale. In two weeks the place was sold.

There was great rejoicing in our house the day the deed was passed. Now, after a half year of planning, repairing, negotiating, and selling, and after three and one-half years in the country, we had at last whittled down the farm to a size we could handle. And we still had the house, the rural life, and the mountain view.

We even went so far, in our celebration, as to go to town to the movies that night. Such squandering of time had not been possible to us for more than two years. At last we were free.

Free of worry, too. The mortgage was retired, the one hundred and sixty acres that now comprised Gaston Hall were free and clear; taxes henceforth were cut by four-fifths. Insurance, general overhead, labor costs, all were proportionately reduced, and plenty of young steers were on the farm to make a new start. We had trimmed our capital investment in what remained to us, including the great house, to an insignificant figure. And still to come, as a return of our capital, was the revenue from the sale of our purebred herd—no mean item.

That night, returning from the movies, we went to our refuge, the front porch. By special dispensation the children, who should long ago have been in bed, rushed excitedly about the lawn, pursuing fireflies. The katydids and tree toads, usually annoying, tonight made joyous racket in the woods. The world, with all its creatures, was at that moment wonderful.

I explained to Margaret, who does not grasp financial matters readily unless it is to her distinct advantage to do so, what the various sales of land meant to us, not only in tremendously reduced capital outlay but also in future operating costs and personal physical effort. I made the story as dramatic as possible. She did not respond as well as I thought she might, so I went from drama to melodrama.

"We have this place in such shape now," I said, "that we could walk off and leave it, if we wanted to, without getting hurt."

At last she registered the proper appreciation.

"You're kidding!" she exclaimed.

"No, really," I said. "See for yourself." I went in the house and returned with all the figures, which I had that day neatly recapitulated, down to the last ten cents.

She looked them over carefully, though what she made of them I do not know, since she cannot even balance her checkbook from month to month. She certainly got the idea, however.

"That's wonderful!" she said. Her eyes glowed. She leaped up impetuously, and I thought she was about to reward me with a kiss. I held out my hands as she approached, and she took them.

"Know something?" she asked coquettishly.

"No, what?" I said, playing up to her gay mood. I began to think how I would respond when she said, "I love you."

Her fingers tightened in mine.

"I'm going right out and buy a new dining-room table," she exclaimed. "We can afford it, now."

CHAPTER FOURTEEN

P LANS long held in abeyance, and new inspirations, were set in motion, all designed to make life easy for us, for a change, instead of the cattle. We could plan with decision, knowing that, for better or worse, we were settled permanently at Gaston Hall.

Our recent experience had taught us more than one lesson, the most important being that, under the nabob influence of seven hundred acres and the conceit that we were country gentlemen, we had crowded out of mind those values we had found in our Argentine friend which, at the time of our introduction to them, had seemed important to us. Cutting down the farm also cut us down to our proper size. As I, at thirty, having written twelve novels no publisher would accept, had stopped fancying myself an undiscovered Nobel Prize winner and had settled down to write within my limitations, so now at forty I determined to adjust myself within my capacity to live.

We had lumps in our throats, Margaret and I, when the great bull Bando left the farm, but it was a sentimental emotion. Actually we were delighted to pass along to Bando's new owner all the griefs and worries of purebred cattle which symbolically departed the farm with him. I had no lachrymose moment, however, when the cowherd was dispersed. It had represented too much fruitless labor. The aches departed from my back with its going. I felt free.

Much as Margaret and I had prepared ourselves for the shrinkage of our acres and our establishment, our pride was hurt. No one likes to fail at anything even when, as in our case, failure actually constituted an improvement in our condition. We wondered especially what the community would think. I was self-conscious for a time in the company of successful farmers. This clumsiness gave way, under the impact of a hundred mounting satisfactions, until we could see that it had not been pride at all, but a cancerous false pride, that had nearly consumed the healthy tissue of our existence.

We discovered that we had not lost face among our neighbors. They were long accustomed to the spree of newcomers who talked big about farming, accomplished little, and eventually sold out and returned "up north." Realizing that despite our failure we loved the countryside so much that we could not leave it, they began to show us more friendliness than before. And we, reorganizing our standards, had time and the openness of mind to appreciate the life available to us in a rediscovery of ourselves, our children, and our acquaintances.

As in a home after housecleaning, we hauled our debris to the trash pile and readied our house for a fresh start. And as every family resolves, at such a time, never again to clutter up the attic with old magazines or the basement with bottles, with like determination Margaret and I put two avowals on the line.

We resolved that in future we would not bite off more than we could chew. Never again would we be guilty of the mistake of overreaching. Translated into action, this meant downscaling the elaborate plans that remained for the house and grounds, particularly. We would leave the woodsy park behind the house as nature intended it, a haven for birds and wildflowers, with only a modest cultured garden planted to shrubs and perennials. We would throw away the landscape gardener's project for refurbishing the front entrance and let the place appear without what it was within, a farmhouse, not a mansion. All this we did zestfully, conscious (perhaps even smugly so) that we were being sensible.

Since we were cutting down, we also decided that our family was large enough. We had talked earlier of a family of nine. In the realism of our present mood we faced up to our limitations as parents, recognized that we had not given Lampert, now nearing five, and Laurie, a year younger than her brother, the attention, love, and affection that they deserved. We resolved to repair that deficiency in ourselves. We could love two, but so help us, nine would be too many. An engineer, building a bridge, weighs tolerances to the last thousandth of an inch. The same engineer, in matrimony, begets offspring without, as a rule, calculating in advance his tensile strength as a parent. Two children appeared to Margaret and me to tax the limits of our strength. We are not sufficiently gifted, in patience and unselfishness, to cope with, let alone master, the myriad dislocations caused by an abundant brood. For some time we had been employing a nursemaid; we decided to take her place. The children had been eating in another room; we brought them to our own table. We four became at last a family.

Lampert began to ride the tractor with me, and help to throw down hay to the steers. When I repaired fences, he worked beside me with his own hammer. Previously I could not spare the time this sharing required; time was too scarce for all that must be done. Now we could be leisurely together. He began to talk to me as we worked, and I enjoyed the philosophy of his growth, the expanding awareness of his mind, the broad reaches of his personality. I became proud of him, not just fond of him.

Laurie, younger and a more complex individual, preferred her mother's company to mine. She was suspicious of my efforts to become acquainted with her, remembering no doubt her earlier overtures toward me which had been repulsed. She was quick to realize that her good opinion had suddenly become important to me, and capitalized on it. Her fee for humoring my awakened interest was a piratical tribute in gum, lollypops, and ice-cream cones, which she extracted from me with all the aplomb of a lawyer securing his retainer—in advance.

I did everything within my means to break her down, to gain an easy and affectionate footing with her. She would have none of me, except by tribute. Even at the age of four, a woman once scorned is a recalcitrant creature.

I had about despaired of winning her confidence when a miracle of nature came to my assistance. Our farm dog, an old English sheep dog named Pandora, who is so devoted to me that she will take orders from no one else, presented me one day with a litter of puppies. Laurie made the discovery. She had found the babies under the front porch. From that moment she was their foster mother. She gave them names: Winken, Blinken, Me Too, Sleepy, Honeybunch, and Poo, and was very serious about their welfare. She encountered some opposition to the adoption from Pandora, and here Laurie had to call on me for help.

In Laurie's mind I became associated with this brood of wonderful snuggly creatures. I gained stature in her sight. The third day of their lives, Laurie and I moved the puppies from their birthplace to a warm shelter in the garage.

Jointly and with gravity we settled all the puppy problems as they arose. I was not a father forcing my attentions upon her, but a colleague in a miraculous enterprise. As the babies grew, so did the comradeship between Laurie and me, and when the pups all left the farm for new homes, Laurie and I were on intimate terms at last. I was rewarded

by the full impact of an affectionate nature as soft as that of her mother, a surprising skill with her hands, and quickness of intellect. She was not a problem any more; she was the unfolding of feminine nature within my house, the source to me of much more satisfaction than the hundred calves which formerly had received most of my attention.

As a family, we began to have picnics on the lawn, to go to town, to gather wild strawberries. The children were assigned chores, and performed them well under the impetus of the jocular admonition, "If you don't work, you don't eat." By association with the children, Margaret and I became aware of their needs: a wading pool, a pair of swings, climbing apparatus.

Riding his tricycle one day, Lampert fell and cracked his head, requiring six stitches. I held his hand while the doctor sewed him up. Lampert, his eyes on me, did not whimper. When the job was done, he piped up strongly, "I like Doctor Scott." The look that passed between the physician and me was mutually satisfying. The little fellow, sustained by the security of the family, had been unafraid. This was a far day from the previous year when this same child had screamed, out of control, over the administration of a simple hypodermic. Doctor Scott arose beaming after Lampert's remark, and was equally gallant. "There will be no charge for this visit," he said. What he might have added, and I think what he implied, was that the Spence family had come a long way. And we had, father even further than son.

Freedom from pressure asserted itself in other ways than in our relations with the children. We began to enjoy incidents that previously would have annoyed us. For some time the stable had been disreputable, littered with trash and wasted feed, with nothing in its accustomed place. One Saturday rain fell and the hands retired to the barn to loaf until pay-off time at noon. In my new leisure, I was able to keep an eye on them, and so put them to work cleaning the stable. Even Glee grumbled at what he considered a useless occupation, but I pointed out that the men were doing nothing else anyway. For three hours Glee, Benny, and I swept, polished, and ordered up the premises until at noon they would have passed an army inspection. I called

Glee, stood off a bit and said triumphantly, "Well, now, what do you think?" He scrutinized our handiwork, hitched up his trousers, looked me in the eye, and said laconically, "A waste of time, if you ask me." A month before, I should have been exasperated at this retort; now I was amused.

About the same time my best hand, easy-going, genial Benny, drifted off without giving notice. A few days later I met him about sundown walking the road to his house in the woods adjacent to my property.

"I haven't seen you this week, Benny," I said.

"No," he answered. "I'm over next door, helping with the spring planting. They pays five dollars a day and give me a side of meat." Benny had been getting four dollars a day from me.

"Is it permanent work?" I asked, glad to see Benny get ahead.

"Five, six days, that's all."

"Then what will you do?"

This was a challenge he had not expected. He took off his leather cap, scratched his head solemnly, shuffled his feet, and grinned. With thirty dollars in his pocket and a few pounds of pork in the kitchen, he had no worries at all.

"Well," he explained cheerfully, "I won't have to work at all for a while."

A year previously I should have pointed out to Benny the insecurity of his existence. Now I accepted his way of life.

By far the most satisfying result of our new adjustment was the confidence that returned to Margaret and me. No longer was every decision vital to our mutual survival. Rather, our problems broke down, in most cases, into individual perplexities. The natural result was a division of responsibilities. So complete became our mutual trust that we began what soon became a refrain in our house. Posed with a question, the one interrogated was likely to reply, "That's in your department," or "That's your problem."

This was not an attempt to evade responsibility to the group. Rather it was an expression of complete trust in the ability of the other.

New problems arose every day now, for in the security of permanent residence, Margaret had begun, with the accumulated vigor of three years of waiting, to redecorate her house. She started in the front hall, and I kept out of it. Everything Margaret undertakes along this line comes out exactly right—ultimately. But anguish attends the birth of her interior decorations.

She did have a vexation in that hall. The foyer runs entirely through the middle of the structure, tying together the front and back porches. The front porch is huge, protected by a dormer that is supported on concrete columns sixty feet high. Double doors are flanked by glass panels and surmounted by a sunburst window. The back porch is also large, with six columns holding up its roof, and with an ornate wooden railing hemming its floor. The doorway here is an exact duplicate of the front façade. North light pours into the hall from the front, southern sun bursts into the hall from the rear. These high lights collide in the center of the hall where, to complicate the situation, there is a black marble mantel. Any wallpaper that is elegant in the north light is pale in the southern sunshine, and a wall paint that softens the garish flood of light from the two sunbursts becomes, in mid-hall by the black mantel, sepulchrally gloomy.

Mastering such a puzzle was a delight to Margaret. For months she reveled in the challenge of it. She would sit in the hall, knees folded like a yogi, inundated by books on interior decoration, contemplating the conflicting light patterns on walls and ceilings, all the while idly drawing pictures of ladies with Victorian coiffures on a large sheet of paper. She consulted textbooks on such subjects as making rooms look smaller, or larger, or lower-ceilinged, or higher-ceilinged, or wide or narrow, until to my inept eyes interior decoration appeared to be a trick of prestidigitation rather than a furnisher's art. She pounced on every new magazine in the mail, thumbing it for pictures, tearing out entire pages which usually had, on the reverse side, the end of an article in which later I became interested.

Once or twice I sought hints concerning the trend of her thinking by examining these excisions from periodicals. The inventory merely intensified my confusion. The hall seemingly bore no relation to this junk, which included a picture of the lounge in Pittsburgh's Duquesne Club, a black Georgian sofa against an anemic yellow backdrop, a small dog of no fixed breed, a Man of Distinction against a walnut panel, a boy fishing in a mountain stream, an article entitled "Make Your Dining Room Look Good Enough to Eat," and several clippings from *Vogue* of stylish living rooms.

"What," I asked one day in dismay, "has all this claptrap to do with your problem?"

Margaret looked vague.

"This Man of Distinction, for example," I said. "What's he doing in our front hall?"

"Oh, him," she replied casually. "He has nothing to do with it. I just liked his looks."

Often I would find Margaret squatting before the black mantel, squinting, her eyes slits, a Texolite color chart in one hand, a pencil in the other. Nervously biting the eraser of her pencil, she would stare into the north corner for a long time, impervious even to such blatant interruptions as a telephone or a demanding child. This business went on at all hours, in varying intensities of light: in the morning of a sunny day, at midmorning of a gloomy day, at noon, in the gentle sunlight of a summer afternoon, or the hard coldness of snow-reflected winter. She set up lamps, turned them on and off, changed bulbs, fussed with the chandelier.

One day I entered the hall to find that changes had been made. Six different colors of paint were swabbed about the walls, wallpaper books with open pages embellished tables, chairs, and mantel. Three rugs were partially unrolled. In the midst of this turmoil sat my yogi wife, doodling her Victorian ladies on a pad of paper. As I entered, she arose.

"Isn't it wonderful!" she said, and retired lightly to the kitchen, leaving me alone amid the tumult of color.

"What's wonderful?" I asked, following her to the gas stove.

"The hall."

"Well," I said, "if you say so, I guess it is. But since you ask, I might as well admit that none of those colors does anything to the hall, so far as I can see."

"That's just the point," she said, flipping lamb chops from a skillet. "Call the children to lunch."

A week later I discovered the cause of her elation. The painters had arrived, and with them the paperhangers. None of the dozen or so papers that had been tested was being put up, nor was the woodwork any color I had seen under scrutiny. Everything was new.

"How do you know this is what you want?" I asked, not doubting Margaret's wisdom, but merely seeking information. "You didn't test this combination at all."

"No," she admitted. "I tried everything else, so this must be it."

So it turned out to be. There was only one slight difficulty involved, about which Margaret was, to my mind, crassly indifferent. On the hall she had spent the entire budget we had set up for redecorating the whole house. I did not press the point, however. It was in her department.

A few days later, working indoors with the two children at play outside my window, I heard a snatch of conversation that brought home to me to what ends we had carried this division of authority.

Said Laurie, nearly four, to her brother: "Lampert, how am I going to get down out of this tree?"

Said Lampert, nearly five: "That's your problem."

CHAPTER FIFTEEN

WHILE Margaret was busy redecorating the hall, I had not been idle. During the two years since my return from the army, I had done nothing about Margaret's formidable repair list with its ominous printed title: TROUBLE!!! Insecure concerning our farm future, I had, secretly at least, expected to pass this list on to a new owner of Gaston Hall.

Now that our residence was permanent, I could no longer delay the long-needed reconstruction. The impending spring rains, which in this region are heavy, would greatly extend the already dangerous damage.

Even so I procrastinated, taking an overlong time to complete the writing of a new book. The real reason for my delay did not concern the book, however, but my own manual deficiency. I had never been able to use my hands. In grammar school, where manual training was compulsory, I had once made a shoe shining box, over the mortise and tenon joints of which I had spent many unhappy hours. My creation was the only product of the class not exhibited on Parent-Teachers' Day. When I took it home, as a Christmas present for my father, he packed it off to the attic. In adulthood I was extremely conscious of my manual clumsiness. Upon our return from South America, for example, Margaret would take a nail from my hands after watching my ineffectual fuddling, and drive it in with the heel of her slipper.

A farm is no place for such ungainliness. The man of the house, in the country, must be the janitor. With the nearest plumber, carpenter, or mason miles away, even the simplest repair, done professionally, costs fifteen to twenty dollars. It therefore behooves the farmer to be the official fixer, attending to dripping faucets, broken electric cords, clogged toilets, unhinged cupboard doors, and the mouse nest in an unused closet. From agility in these simple occupations, he must go on then to major undertakings in all the fields of everyday craftsmanship.

In our new program of self-sufficiency and self-reliance, the time had come for me to learn these crafts. For, as Margaret often reiterated, my time was no longer consumed with urgent farm work, and I had leisure to make of handiwork an absorbing and money-saving hobby.

The most urgent needs were a dry basement and a tight roof over the west wing. The roof looked less formidable, so I tackled it first. It was a nearly flat surface some forty by seventy feet, covered with copper sheeting. The seams were open in nineteen places, through which rain coursed in such volume that the plaster below had already fallen. With blow torch, caulking compound, and roof cement I mended the open seams, with gratifying results. The first hard rain of the season did not penetrate the roof at all, so Glee and I replastered the ceiling.

Buoyed by this success, I invaded the basement. A new cloudburst came along, during which I descended to the nether regions in rubber boots and charted the unwelcome rivulets. The walls seeped water in a dozen places. Cataracts caught in window wells poured through rotted sills, and

169

rushed about the basement floor seeking outlet. Four floor drains at strategic places, evidently designed to draw off surface water, did not function. In fact, they bubbled as though water made ingress through them, rather than exit.

The children, helping me to study my problem, had a hilarious time. They sailed boats. The basement is more than one hundred feet long, with a concrete-paved central hall. Lampert discovered that a raft would cruise almost the full length of the hall, from a high point in the furnace room to a door which led out into a brick-walled drying court. I noticed that his raft passed most swiftly over the floor drains, clearly indicating that water made entry through them in substantial volume. Obviously, this flow must be reversed first of all.

At the first break in the weather, with the aid of a plumber's lead line, I probed the hidden recesses of the drains. I discovered that the system which drew rainfall from the house roof converged into a single six-inch sewer pipe laid under the basement floor, emptying into a creek east of the house. Evidently the cellar floor had been paved at a later date, covering up the drain line. At a still later date, probably after the basement became leaky, holes had been cut in the concrete to connect with the main sewer. This drain had become clogged somewhere, so that all the rain which collected on the roof backed up into the basement. I located the congestion and freed it. Immediately the surface water drained away, much to Lampert's disappointment.

The seepage through the foundation was also curable. I built a new drainage system outside the house to draw water away from the walls, digging up half the lawn in the process. Fortunately, or so I thought at the time, a hard freeze occurred, rather than more rain, during this ditching work.

Now the chain reaction which had necessitated one expenditure after another on the farm exploded in the house. Since the lawn was torn up anyway, Glee and I graded up a section of the back yard in which Margaret desired a flower garden. We finished this chore just ahead of a deluge.

I was in town when the big rain began, and mentally congratulated myself on making the house dry ahead of it. In fact, I welcomed the storm as a good test of my repairs.

A harassed wife awaited me on my return home. She looked as though someone had hit her with a sack of flour.

"What on earth!" I exclaimed.

"You and your repairs," she replied, and led me to the ballroom. All my plaster had come down on a newly placed rug and furniture. Margaret had been in the middle of the room, emptying buckets, when it had fallen. Water flowed from the ceiling and shimmered down the walls.

"Take a deep breath," Margaret said, and conducted me to the basement. The floor crawled with inches of water.

Eventually, after calling in an expert to do the job over at a cost of seven hundred dollars, I found out what had happened. As for the roof, the hard freeze of the previous week had reopened all my mended seams, and since I had repaired the plaster, there was no outlet through which the rain could drip. It had in consequence spread over the entire ceiling, bringing the plaster down. In the basement, my work had been better. In fact, the contractor found no fault with it. He had plenty to say, however, about my grading job on the back lawn. Glee and I had made a catch basin for all the rain that fell in the back park, an area of eight acres, and then conveniently had set the low point of this grading just outside the house foundation. Water pressure, piling up in the man-made lake, had blown a hole three feet wide in the wall.

After the contractors had departed, their fee made me well aware of the necessity for economy in the future. A large pile of sand and gravel remained from the repair work, and I determined to make use of it. For some time Margaret and I had considered converting an English-type clothes-drying court, surrounded by a high brick wall, into a garage, since our car was stored in a shed three hundred yards from the house. This court actually was an extension of the house itself, with an opening into the basement. To my unskilled eye, by simply extending brickwork and adding a roof, we might have a two-car garage. And the sand and gravel were already at hand. Here was an opportunity for economy not to be missed.

As usual, there was a problem: where to find the antique pink brick, slightly under standard size, of which the house had been built. Matching the brick was important, since the wall would be visible from both the front lawn and the back garden. Margaret, always helpful in such a crisis and also quick to capitalize on one, now took matters firmly in hand. The brick in the old water tower was identical with that in the house.

"But that's the reservoir for the house, barns, water troughs, and the hog lot," I said. "We can't tear that down."

"The time has come," Margaret said in a tone defying contradiction, "to get rid of that wheezy old gasoline pump and give ourselves a respectable water supply. The hardest job we have around here is cranking that engine and running madly up and down hill turning valves. We're going to have an electric pump."

This sounded sensible, except that as soon as we converted to a pressure system, Margaret would no doubt want shower baths all over the house, and hose connections in the garden and under the porches, and goodness knows what else.

Shower baths would lead to remodeling of the bathrooms, with expensive new fittings and probably tile floors. Undoubtedly Margaret's suggestion was merely a left jab, concealing the solid right-hand punch of staggering improvements that would be, to her mind, a logical development once the water supply was modernized. Little I knew then that what was really in her mind was a tea house and fountain in her new garden. This, by a devious syllogism, ultimately emerged as a logical conclusion from the two premises of garage and electric pump.

The chain reaction of spending was in full operation, however, so Glee and I set to work to pull down the water tower and install an electric pump. This would cause the house to be without water for a week, and Margaret could not ignore this opportunity to hold me to an old promise.

"We've been here four years and I haven't been to New York yet," she reminded me. "You promised me that trip, and since there's no water in the house, I think I'll pack up and go right now."

She had completed her renovations of the front hall and was turning her attention to the dining room, library, and two upstairs bedrooms. Smarting under the expensive water installation now before me, I concluded hurriedly that I would save money by financing a trip to New York rather than redecorating three rooms. Besides, I had seen in the county paper the advertisements for two big antique auctions the following week, which Margaret must also have noticed.

"All right," I said. "I think that's a fine idea."

This time, much to her surprise, Margaret actually got away. In her absence, Glee and I installed the pump, then scraped clean all the brick from the old tower.

Now all that remained was to build the garage. Every

workman, of course, requires a helper, presumably to hand him tools, but actually to do the dirty work. For this purpose I engaged the services of a jackleg artisan roughly skilled in all the handicrafts and renowned the county over for his resourcefulness in masonic improvisation. His name is Willie Moss. He is a Negro of some three hundred thirty pounds of brawn and muscle, capped by a cheery face in which dangles a stringy mustache. He is a jovial man, but withal cautious, particularly where the white man is concerned. Although I, Iowa born and New York trained, see no reason to judge any man otherwise than on his merits, a fact Willie was quick to discover, he would not contradict me in any detail of my proposed garage construction, even though he knew much, and I little, about this type of work. He had lived among white Southerners too long for life-time habits to be abated.

I outlined my construction plan and asked his advice. He was surprised at my question, then decided it was merely rhetorical.

"Le's get on wit it, den," he said.

The brick work was easy. With Willie to line up the courses and give the mortar the proper consistency and tote all the brick, we made a good team. His eyes danced with merriment the whole time, especially as I made a great fuss of bossing the job whenever Glee appeared. But he never once broke down and laughed. When I went indoors, as I did often, to answer the telephone or get a glass of water, Willie made miraculous changes in the work during my absences.

As the hours passed, a tacit understanding grew up between us. By now we had come to the more complicated roof structure, where skill in carpentry is important. Confounded by a problem, I did not ask Willie's advice. In-

174

stead, I made a telephone call. When I returned, Willie had accomplished his magic in the proper manner. He was always apologetic about this.

"I di'n' want to loaf while yo' wuz gone," he would say.

The time came when the ridge pole was to be raised, and Willie quietly made preparations for erecting a scaffold. I could see no reason for such labor. After all, the roof was not large, and certainly not heavy. We could tack up the rafters, I suggested, then climb up carefully and drive thirty penny nails into them and save ourselves half a day of work. Willie looked dubious.

"A'ri'," he agreed.

We set to work. All went well. The rafters appeared to be seating sturdily, certainly with enough strength to bear my hundred and fifty pounds at the critical moment. The long pole was measured and sawed, shored into place with a pair of two-by-fours. I crawled, catlike, with hammer and nails, to make the ridge pole firm at the ends. I had not made two strokes of the hammer before Willie stopped me. He had never done anything like that before, so I knew the matter was important.

"Nein," he said. Willie's English has unique syllables.

"What's wrong?"

Willie wouldn't say. He looked perplexed. His black eyes shimmered with amusement. Sweat irrigated his brow as he fought for self-control. He could not tell me, a white man, what to do. Instead, he motioned me to descend, handed me the four-by-four prop with which he had supported my weight aloft, and himself began cautiously to climb to the peak. There is a difference between one hundred fifty pounds and three hundred thirty, particularly when the lesser weight is supporting the greater. My helper's bulk teetered over my head. I strained to keep him up there.

Cautiously he raised his hammer and brought it down. The shock of the blow tore the shoring stick from my hands. Down came the ridge pole, the rafters, and Willie, all on top of me.

I went into the house and called the doctor, who treated me for lacerations. I did not return to work that day. When, next morning, I hobbled out to suggest to Willie that I hire him a helper, he was on top of a newly built scaffold, his mouth full of nails, pounding down the composition shingles.

He looked most apologetic, but his eyes laughed out loud.

"I di'n' want to loaf while yo' wuz gone," he said.

We had only a half day's work left on the garage, consisting of painting the wood trim, when I heard the telephone ring in the house and ran to answer it. Margaret was calling from New York.

"Has my new wallpaper arrived?" she inquired.

"What wallpaper?"

"The wonderful paper I bought here in New York. Didn't you get my letter?"

"Not yet."

"Well—I found the most marvelous papers you ever saw at an interior decorator's closing-out sale. It was the chance of a lifetime. I can hardly wait to get at those three rooms."

"Oh," I groaned.

"I'll be home in the morning."

"But I thought you were going to take a good long holiday?"

"I'd rather be at home," she said. "It's really not much fun here."

Her first action, on arrival, was to inspect the new garage. Willie was cleaning up his paint brushes, preparatory to departing from my payroll at noon. At least, I thought, this expense was ended, anyway.

But I was wrong. Margaret's eyes caught a large pile of brick, taken down from the water tower but left over from the garage.

"Are those extras?" she asked.

"Yes'm," said Willie.

"Wonderful," Margaret said. "When you get through with the garage, Willie, don't you dare hire to anyone else for a while. I want you to build a brick wall around my new garden."

Definitely, from my point of view, Margaret's vacation had not been a success.

She returned gaily to the house, and turned on a water faucet in the kitchen. The firm, gushing pressure, after the gravity idling of water heretofore, was very impressive. Margaret's eyes sparked again.

"Is it this way all over the house?"

"There's not enough pressure," I lied, making a hasty exit, "for a shower bath upstairs."

CHAPTER SIXTEEN

WITH the coming of the spring of 1948, beginning our fifth year on the farm, when the redbud and dogwood were in full flower in the woods and crocuses decked the lawn, Margaret had another of her logical ideas.

All winter she had been doing the cooking and housekeeping unassisted, an arduous chore in a thirty-room dwelling, even when eighteen of those rooms are in the basement. In her exposition of this new theme to me, she minimized her own travail, concentrating, as befits a practical spouse, on her husband's welfare. She recalled to my mind the laborious hours I had spent the previous summer in a vain effort to keep the lawns neat, and reminded me that the bareness of the canning cupboard necessitated a large vegetable garden. Therefore, said she, why not hire a couple: a man to garden, scrub, and take off my back the "little fixings" around the house; a woman to cook and clean and, possibly, act as a baby sitter in the evenings. If we were sincere about putting the farm to work for us, here certainly was an excellent place to start.

I agreed. Nothing annoys me so much as mowing lawns, except fixing leaky toilets. And I had suspected for some weeks that this year I would be compelled, for lack of an alibi, to go to work raising vegetables, a most disagreeable

178

prospect. Far better, I reasoned, to earn the salary of a couple by writing magazine articles than to renew my acquaintance, in the garden, with an aching back. We advertised for a couple.

Promptly, in reply, came a man about forty years old who, from his rustic haircut, certainly looked the gardener. He was big of frame, kind of eye, soft-spoken, and obviously intelligent. He was good with vegetables, he said, had tended lawns, and was also handy with poultry. This last attribute was a real attraction, since all our feathered friends die promptly the moment I minister to them. His name was Sephus.

I liked him at once. He had no references, but his honest brown eyes were recommendation enough. Here was a man who would earn his hire. I did not quite like what I saw sitting in a battered old Stutz with New Hampshire license plates in which Sephus had driven to the farm. A bird-faced little woman, whose sharp eye and sharper ear had taken in every detail of our conversation and several times had squeezed together the thin, brittle line of her mouth when Sephus had fumbled for words, looked now from the car directly at me. She was older, by a good span, than her companion. There was no kindness in her darting eye, though a strong hint of a bright mind furiously at work. At my invitation, she descended from the vehicle, not at all for me to evaluate, but to pass judgment on me.

"I am Mrs. Portius," she said, with the full-steamed condescension of a dowager interviewing a prospective chauffeur. Her clothes contradicted her regal manner, but of this she was unconscious. She wore a black cloth coat with a rabbit collar that had seen too much rain, and a short blue dress with a white starched collar such as adorns maids in ostentatious households. Her lumpy legs, obviously harassed by varicose veins, were covered by brown lisle stockings, one of which hung down to the calf, having escaped an uncooperative garter. Her shoes were of the health-cult type, built for comfort, and new. She was quite small, beside towering Sephus appearing even smaller, and as I looked at her hands and face I wondered whether she could possibly be this strong man's wife or was, perhaps, his mother instead. Blue veins stood out on her well-worn hands, her face was amply wrinkled, and there was a triple ring of loose flesh at her throat. Her hair was almost white, cut short in a ragged sort of bob which she nervously threw back, from time to time, across her ears.

She was a competent cateress, she said in a metallic, aggressive voice. She was accustomed to running a large household. She knew exactly what would be expected of her in a "ménage" (her pronunciation of the word was very French) the size of ours. Here she swept her gnarled hands to include the whole spacious front of the house. Her bird-like eyes, which had not ceased darting for a moment, now lit on a tricycle on the porch, and she said, "How many children?"

"Two."

"I am also a competent nursemaid," she told me, "and I shall prefer to be called 'Nurse' around the house."

With that I called Margaret and went to my study. I did not want the responsibility of turning Mrs. Portius away. Ten minutes later, when the old Stutz rattled away, I discovered that the Portius couple had been hired.

"I think they will work out all right," Margaret said, in what sounded to me like a strong effort to convince herself of that fact. "Mrs. Portius is a bit bossy, but I can put up with that if she takes some of the work off my shoulders."

I shrugged.

"Oh, there's just one thing," Margaret added. Her voice was anxious.

"Yes?"

"They have two hundred pullets they want to feed out to laying size, when they'll be able to sell them at a good price."

"Not on my feed, I hope."

"No, they'll buy the feed. I told them they could use the old chicken coop behind the swimming pool."

"Well—I don't like it, but I guess there's nothing I can do."

"And they have three goats."

"Goats, for heaven's sake?"

"Yes. They eat health foods or something, and drink goat's milk."

"Where do you propose to house the goats?"

"They also go behind the swimming pool. There is a big patch of poison ivy there, and Mrs. Portius says they'll eat it all off for us. They love poison ivy. And she says it's a myth that goats smell. Just billy goats and they don't have a billy goat."

"What else?" I asked. People with goats and chickens would have other things.

"Two dogs, but they'll keep them chained up, out of sight."

"And?"

"Well—I hardly knew what to do about this, but having gone that far . . ."

"Yes?"

"Sephus sleeps in a trailer. He likes fresh air. So he's going to park his own car and trailer in the woods and sleep there."

"What do you mean, his own car and trailer? Are they a two-car family?"

"I guess so. I'm not real sure. And they have some furniture that we'll have to store."

From Margaret's tone I knew this was the last item on the list.

"How much?"

"I don't know, but there's plenty of storage room in the basement, now that it doesn't leak any more."

The next morning a large moving van, followed by the Stutz, followed by a vivid green Essex runabout drawing a home-made trailer, followed by a truck containing crates of chickens and the goats, convoyed up to the front door and Mrs. Portius descended upon us. All day, and most of the night, she was moving in. The trailer had to be moved twice. The first time Sephus had lodged it too close to a tree, and Mrs. Portius feared it might be struck by lightning. The second time I ordered it moved; it was within ten feet of the back porch. The basement rooms did not suit our housekeeper for the furniture storage; they were too dark. So the stuff was piled in large heaps in the third floor hall. Considerable fencing was required to satisfy her that her pullets would be contained, and she fussed over the lack of shelter for her goats. About midnight, the kitchen light still on, I went to suggest that she and Sephus had better retire, but Mrs. Portius had the first word.

"I might as well let you know right now," she attacked me, "that I work best when people stay out of my kitchen. I'll oblige you to remember that."

"But it is very late. Hadn't you better go to bed?"

"I can't," she said. "I have to fix the oatmeal."

"The oatmeal? We don't eat oatmeal often," I said. "You don't need to stay up on our account."

"I'm not," she said. "Sephus must have his oatmeal at five every morning, so I cook it at night. It takes three hours."

We, who use bottled gas for cooking, are as sparing of it as possible, but somehow I did not think this the proper moment to bring up the subject.

"Well, I'll see you in the morning," I said, backing out, and giving silent Sephus a searching glance as I departed.

"Do," she said.

I was halfway upstairs when she rushed from the kitchen.

"Another thing," she said. "I do the talking for Sephus and me. I also take the money, so on payday give me one check, made out to cash. That's right, isn't it, Sephus?"

No sound from the kitchen.

"Sephus!" Her voice took on a nagging note, one to which evidently her vocal chords, and Sephus's ears, were alike well attuned. He appeared in the doorway.

"Isn't that right?" she repeated. I knew that he had not heard her question.

"Yes, yes," he said softly, "perfectly right."

Despite this introduction, the Portius team went to work next day with vigor. Sephus was up at five, and had milked his goats and fed his chickens before the house was astir. Breakfast was bountiful, with bacon as well as eggs, and hot biscuits. Mrs. Portius had insisted, however, on a more simple fare for the children, whom she took from our table and placed in a housekeeper's room off the kitchen where, she said, "they can spill milk without ruining any rugs."

Sephus went to work at once on the lawns. He knew exactly what to do. He hunted up Glee and together they readied the vegetable gardens for planting. This done, he cleaned up the debris of leaves and trash remaining from the winter, swept the walks, and scrubbed the porches.

After breakfast, Margaret and Mrs. Portius had a conference that lasted a long time. A number of rules, all framed by our new housekeeper, were laid down, and meals

183

were planned for several days. Mrs. Portius's duties were defined, and at her own suggestion she accepted other responsibilities than those Margaret outlined. She was not, Margaret insisted, to be a nursemaid; but if she would, on occasion, be a baby sitter in the evening, we would be grateful. Mrs. Portius agreed.

She was a nursemaid within the day. She insisted, that night, on putting the children to bed, and Sephus waited a long time in the kitchen for his gluten bread and goat's milk, while she taught the children two new prayers. Sephus made no complaint.

Within a fortnight, Mrs. Portius was, as she liked to point out, indispensable to us. She certainly had taken charge of us. The children were cowed and well-mannered. The dog slunk in for her noonday meal on cautious pads. Margaret never went near the kitchen, and I never went near Mrs. Portius. Sephus was a perfect gardener, and for this I was grateful enough to overlook Mrs. Portius's annoying habit of standing in the dining room, after she had served lunch or dinner, to discuss with us all the household problems and beyond them, exhaustively, her philosophies of life, love, and religion. At first I enjoyed these monologues, for in them certainly there were the eccentric raw materials of fiction. I even considered the prospect that I might pay Mrs. Portius' monthly wages—in checks made out to cash —by writing a series of sketches about her. As days passed, however, the savor departed from her delectable meals, for the monologues continued through every one of them, and no hint, suggestion, or even rudeness, could head them off. She balanced the score one night when guests were present by serving a handsome dinner without a word, and I forgave her previous loquacity.

Each night she had the children on their knees at bed-

184

time, and the prayers she taught them were beautiful and new to me. Rarely was Sephus fed before ten, and oftener the clock pointed to eleven. Yet never a word from him.

I noticed, of course, that Mrs. Portius was working much more strenuously than she had been engaged to do, and several times both Margaret and I tried to relieve her of some of the duties she had taken on herself. She waved us aside peremptorily, and if we pressed the issue she retreated to her kitchen, which we dared not invade. She prepared nine meals a day: three health diets for herself and Sephus, three bland servings for the children, three excellent repasts for Margaret and me. She cleaned the entire house. Cobwebs that had been in corners for months disappeared. She helped Sephus to tend the pullets and the goats, fed and groomed her dogs, and supervised the moral, physical, and spiritual welfare of our two children. Margaret and I were helpless to prevent any of her activities.

The bottled-gas bill leaped from five dollars a month to fifteen, chiefly from the oatmeal.

By the time Sephus brought to the house the first offerings from his vegetable garden, the Portius family was immovably entrenched. Margaret and I had more leisure than ever before, and this was gratifying. Mrs. Portius and I were at odds on three issues, though not belligerently so. I refused to discuss with her, even under the most adroit goading, the comparative merits of her religion, which was a sort of spiritualism, and mine, which she described as "neopagan." She wanted very much to convert both Margaret and me, and implored us to invite down, as a house guest, a spiritualistic medium from Boston who evidently was her friend. The second source of friction was the goat's milk. Several times Mrs. Portius tried to add it to my diet, without success, and she took my refusals as a personal affront. This did not last long, for one noon, after I had drunk my habitual glass of milk, she raked me with her darting eyes and said, "Taste anything wrong with the milk?"

"No," I said.

"No difference at all?"

"Not that I can detect."

She cackled like a Walt Disney witch, jumping up and down, slapping her thighs.

"Goat's milk," she said, greatly enjoying her joke. "It was goat's milk you just drank. Don't ever again tell me it tastes different from any other."

After that, I never knew what I was drinking.

Our third point of issue was more protracted. Mrs. Portius now had decided that she could not part with her chickens. They had long since reached the age at which she had agreed to sell them, but she wanted to keep them and vend the eggs instead. At this I demurred.

"A bargain is a bargain," I repeated, over and over. "You agreed to get rid of them. Now get rid of them."

She did not do so. To spare an argument, I did not press the matter stubbornly, or make a direct issue of it. Then one day, at lunch as usual, Mrs. Portius confronted me with a new proposal. She had ordered two hundred baby chicks. These she proposed, on delivery, to put in the basement until they were old enough to run with the hens.

"No, Mrs. Portius," I said. "Enough is enough. You already have more than you can do, between your farm and mine. I don't want any baby chicks attracting rats to the basement. Definitely you will not bring baby chicks into my house."

She was surprised at the firmness of my decision. She looked at me as though I had grossly insulted her.

"What's a few more chickens added to those I've got?"
she asked.

"You forget that you are disposing of those you have,"
I replied. "And there will—definitely—not be any more."

"But I've already ordered them."

"You can cancel the order."

"I can't do that."

"Had you consulted me in advance, Mrs. Portius, you
know what my answer would have been. Now please, let
us have lunch alone without any more talk."

Mrs. Portius's mouth drooped. Without a word she
whirled about and retired to her kitchen.

"Is she worth all this?" I asked Margaret.

"I can't cope with her any more," Margaret said.

"Sometimes I have the feeling," I went on, "that we are
living in her house, through sufferance."

"How is Sephus doing?"

"Excellently. I couldn't ask for a better man. He works
sensibly, and he never talks."

"I wish the same could be said for his wife," Margaret
said.

"I think you're afraid of her," I remarked facetiously.

"Afraid of her! I'm scared to death. I can't go in my
kitchen. I can't tell my children what to do. I can't move a
chair from one room to another—in my own house!"

"Then is she worth keeping?"

Margaret considered the puzzle thoughtfully. She was
under the heel of a tyrant, but it was a benevolent heel, in
that now she had time to do hundreds of things she had been
trying to accomplish for more than three years. In the
evenings we were free to go out; this alone was not something to be thrown aside lightly.

"I guess we just have to weigh the advantages against the

disadvantages," she said. "She certainly has relieved me of all the responsibilities of my household."

"And taken the children away from you."

Margaret was grim. "Not quite," she said. "They are little angels for her—too angelic, in fact. Sometimes I'm afraid she is taking all the individuality out of them. But they obey her."

"They haven't complained to me."

"They won't, either—because they fear her. But she is wonderful to them in many ways."

"Yes, she is. Well—what does it add up to?"

"She stays, I guess."

Mrs. Portius popped her head in the door, and looked at me.

"Did you do anything about that septic tank?" she asked.

"Please, Mrs. Portius, not while we're eating."

"But I want to know," she said. "Sink is most stopped up, and I suspect the septic tank needs cleaning. I've been telling you that for a week."

Her remark was a deliberate goad. She knew I had been hunting fruitlessly for the septic tank ever since we had moved to the farm, and she also knew that if anything could be calculated to destroy the taste of my meal, the thought of an overflowing sewer would do it.

"What's the use," I said to Margaret, and excused myself. Mrs. Portius returned in triumph to her kitchen. She was square with me.

I had the last word on that subject, as events turned out. Some days later, I was having breakfast when Mrs. Portius descended upon me in a storm cloud.

"If you want to know where your septic tank is," she shouted in a rage, "come and have a look. Sephus is in it —up to his hips."

And so he was. The goats had eaten off most of the clump of poison ivy behind the swimming pool, exposing a half acre of ground which everyone had shunned up to that time. This morning one of the goats had retired to the poison ivy patch to bear a kid, and Sephus had gone to minister to her needs. Within three feet of her, he sank deep into a viscoid muck. The lost was found.

Sephus was inclined to laugh off the incident, but not his consort. She would not go near the poison ivy to help him, and he was afraid to move lest he sink down even deeper. But he was philosophical, and as I approached he volunteered the first remark in many days.

"Well, we don't have to look for it any more," he said.

"Go on in there and get him out," Mrs. Portius commanded me. "Goodness knows what contagion he's getting already."

I went to the house, returned with a long rope, tied one end to a tree, and tossed Sephus the loose end. Poison ivy breaks out on me just from pollen blowing in the wind, and I did not care to rub against it unless Sephus was in real danger. Even while extricating himself, Sephus felt around with his feet, and by the time he was on safe ground he knew the exact dimensions of the tank, that it was made of concrete, and what amount of labor would be required to clean it.

Mrs. Portius cut short his narration of explanation. Shouting as though he was a small child, she told him what to do to rid himself of his clothes. He took several steps toward her, as though to obey, but she withdrew with a squeak of panic.

"Don't you come near me," she fussed.

Sephus deliberately took another step toward her. I think he was enjoying himself immensely, although his face was a stone image. For the first time in his life he had her on the run.

"Eek!" she screamed. "Sephus!"

He walked past her and went to the garage. While he bathed in the basement, she stood at the head of the stairs, adjuring him to use a fresh washcloth for his ears and eyes, to rinse three times in clear running water, and then swab down completely with a mange cure she used on the dogs. Not until he had emerged in fresh clothes did she approach him, and then it was to look in his ears, up his nostrils, and between his fingers and toes to satisfy herself that no uncleanness clung to him.

She could see that I was highly amused, and she had her revenge. All I received for lunch that day was a glass of goat's milk. She was too upset to cook, she said.

A week later some friends from Ohio came on for a fortnight's visit. We are particularly fond of the Cunninghams. We had met them during the war, where we were neighbors in Washington. Gerald, an electronics engineer, has many attributes, chief of them being that he plays aggressive chess and from his knowledge of electronics can repair our radio, something no local professional mechanic will attempt, since it is a complicated prewar model. Gerald never visits us without bringing along his tool kit. Della, his wife, is a gay, lighthearted girl of farm origin who zestfully enjoys rural life, whether it involves a hike across the fields or a long day of peach canning. Their son Dusty is the age of our children. The Cunninghams always give a hearty lift to our household.

This time they also gave a hearty lift, but of another kind, to Mrs. Portius. Della went at once to the kitchen to make herself useful. Mrs. Portius not only repulsed her but misinterpreted Della's gesture and from that moment eyed her with grave suspicion. Further, she could not bully Dusty as she did our children, for he was made of sterner stuff. On the second day of this visit, descending upon the living room to give it the daily dusting, Mrs. Portius stumbled on Gerald, flat on his back, his tools surrounding him. He was repairing the radio. Mrs. Portius told him to get out. He looked up from his work, told her she would have more to clean when he finished, and resumed his labor. She did not know him well enough to reply with any strategic advantage, so she retired. He was her enemy. Her noonday monologue that day was for his exclusive benefit. Subject: Respect for One's Elders.

Whether cooking for three additional persons was the tension that broke the fine mainspring of Mrs. Portius's self-control, or whether the accumulated mountains of labor she had performed for some months finally overburdened her slight and aging frame, I do not know. From tolerable matriarchy she swung sharply onto a course of vindictive shrewishness. Sharply her tongue lashed out at Margaret, at me, and at our guests. Sephus, who tolerated seemingly any of her moods, was compelled to intervene and to remind her, one night, that she was not the mistress of the house. She became enraged, and drove him from the kitchen. I began to understand why he slept in the trailer, deep in the woods. There he had peace.

The next morning, while Margaret, the Cunninghams, and I were at breakfast, Mrs. Portius entered the dining room and began to remove the service.

"Sit here all morning if you like," she snapped, "but I have work to do."

We all withdrew. Gerald and I left the house, inventing

an inspection tour of the farm that would take all morning. A moment later, while we were walking across a field, we saw Mrs. Portius' aged Stutz plod down the road.

At noon we found Della in the hall, in tears. She told her husband to pack their clothes; they were going home. Upstairs I found Margaret, also in tears. She would not talk.

The time had come, I thought, for a showdown with Mrs. Portius. I invaded the kitchen; she was not there. No preparations for lunch were under way. I decided to wait.

Distinctly to my ears then came a faint cheeping, which could only be one thing: baby chicks. The sound came from the basement. I went down the stairs two at a time.

In the laundry room, spread out on tables, were the paraphernalia of the brooder house. In the midst of them, setting watering tins, was Mrs. Portius.

She whirled on me as I entered, but this time I had the first word.

"I thought I said no baby chicks."

"Now you listen to . . ."

"Oh, no," I said quickly, "you listen to me. You have deliberately chosen to ignore me."

As she caught her breath to speak, I held up my hand.

"Not this time," I said. "No arguments at all. Just pack up the whole mess: chickens, chicks, goats, dogs, cars, trailer, and furniture, and go. We'll have to get along without you."

"You don't appreciate all I've . . ."

"Yes, I do, with all my heart. But my wife is in tears, my guest is in tears, and baby chicks are all over the basement. Enough is enough. Get Sephus and go."

As though cued, Sephus came in, a one-hundred-pound sack of starter and growing mash on his back.

"No use setting it down, Sephus," I told him. "There will be no chicks fed in my house."

Sephus turned to go.

"Aren't you going to say anything, Sephus?" Mrs Portius barked. "Are you going to let me be insulted, without offering a word?"

"Time's come to go, ma," Sephus replied.

"I have to get lunch," Mrs. Portius said.

"I'll get lunch," I said. "You pack up and go."

I went upstairs. A few minutes later Sephus came in, to clear his health foods from the refrigerator.

"We won't give you any trouble," he said sadly. "I'm sorry."

"So am I, Sephus," I said. "You've done a fine job and I'll miss you."

"I liked it here," he said. He picked up a jar of goat's milk and an assortment of rye and gluten breads. "Don't think badly of the old lady," he went on. "She's never tried to work for anybody before. It's been hard on her, too. She tried."

"I know she did, Sephus," I said, "and in many ways her work was excellent. It's just too hard an adjustment for all of us to make."

Sephus nodded.

"That's it," he said. "Too much adjustment. I want to tell you something, if I may."

"Of course, Sephus."

"Mrs. Portius was born a very wealthy woman. She never did a day's work until she was fifty-four. That was in 1929, when everything went."

He could see that I was adding eighteen to fifty-four to get her present age.

"That's right," he said. "So don't hold it against her. She's strong-willed, and her pride has been terribly hurt, and this is the first time she's ever worked for anyone—she who has had many employees in her time. It's hard to walk cobble-stones in an old shoe."

"I'm sorry, Sephus," I said. "I didn't understand. If she had just told us, we might have gotten on better."

"Too proud," Sephus said. "You have to admire her, even for trying, at age seventy-two."

"I do admire her," I said sincerely.

"We'll go to chicken farming," Sephus said. "She'll make out very well at that."

"I intend to give you a month's wages, of course."

"Well—good-by. Mrs. Portius will not come in the house again, and we'll be gone by morning." He held out his hand, the first time in four months that he had met me on even terms.

"Tell me, Sephus," I said, "if you will, but don't answer if you don't want to. Are you her husband?"

Sephus smiled.

"Oh, no," he said. "She adopted me out of an orphanage —when I was a child, and she had everything in the world to make me happy."

CHAPTER SEVENTEEN

SOON after the departure of Mrs. Portius and Sephus, the family went walking in the woods and discovered, quite by accident, an ancient formal garden long overgrown with raspberry briars and poison ivy. We had been too busy to uncover this treasure earlier.

Roses still bloomed along the old wires, boxwood lined the faint outline of flower beds. Rank perennials, smothered in ferns, and day lilies, of which there were many varieties, sprawled over the paths, having long since burst the confines of their original plantings.

This garden was entirely surrounded by a pine forest which not only gave the setting the appearance of a Gothic cloister but also filtered and gave acoustics to a breeze overhead. In the midst of the horticultural ruin stood a tall tea house in excellent preservation. This patrician structure had the same cornice and frieze detail, the same colonnades, the same architectural sweep as the main house, and its entrance, reached by three stone steps, was flanked by the same kind of ornamental tiles which I had admired next door in the gardens of James Madison at Montpelier. For twenty years this sanctuary was unnoticed until we, breaking through the underbrush with children and dog, came upon it. We speculated immediately whether other hidden wonders also existed on our property.

We explored the forest, marking a score of holly trees for later moving to the garden. We picnicked by streams the existence of which we had known only vaguely, and much to the children's delight, one creek possessed a sandy bottom ideal for wading.

These outings encouraged us to observe the works of nature. The children spotted bird and squirrel nests, a covey of quail behind the well house, a family of bluebirds under the railroad bridge, honey bees in a red oak tree, and a brown thrush who sang each morning from the peak of a dogwood tree. They found polliwogs and turtles in the old swimming pool, and a woodchuck who made his home in an unused drainage tile. The children were particularly fascinated by the whippoorwills, which spoke English; and they made the discovery that the mockingbird, when not entertaining with impersonations of bird celebrities, has his own enchanting song.

Under such influences, Margaret and I began to relax. The urgencies that previously had exhausted us seemed no longer important. Rid of the pressure of large-scale farm enterprises, our minds were free to react to the benign stimuli of nature and the excitements of the children. As a result, we became aware, before long, that a new tolerance was exerting itself in us. Our subconscious desires, for years forcibly put down, welled up within us and were not repulsed.

This perhaps requires some explanation. What Margaret and I had done in New York and elsewhere was to try to put out of mind the basic needs of the heart. The great expansion of psychiatry in the past decade would indicate that we were not alone in this. In our concentration upon materialism we had put a thin veneer of fashionable walnut over the solid oak beams of healthy living. As a veneer merely hides from public view what is still basically underneath, we had changed nothing, merely concealed it. The standards of our time, accenting material wealth, friendship for the sake of business, wittiness rather than understanding, brilliance rather than permanence, are impositions of the mind, not of the heart, certainly not of the soul.

Yet in the city to be a sophisticate appears to be the necessity of age and the dream of youth. Our most successful lecturers and writers are, in the main, the smoothest sophisticates. The dictionary warns us that to sophisticate anything is to adulterate it, to falsify, to make artificial, to debase, spoil, or corrupt. Therefore our emulation is based on a false foundation.

The conscious mind may accept such a standard, but the subconscious cannot and will not do so. Contempt by the mind for the basic hungers of the soul is a tragic intolerance, since it sets up a conflict within the individual, and makes man at war with himself. Under such stress, happiness is impossible.

Rather than admit, however, that there is still within us a yearning after the fundamental values of existence, an admission that would strip off our veneer, we refuse to face up to the struggle within ourselves and seek solace in the psychiatrist. Within the pattern of sophistication perhaps he can arrange an armistice between the warring factions of our being. Of course he cannot do so, any more than he can compromise our sex drive. While he might set us upon the road to inner security, we will not accept his conclusions for they would entail modification of our so-called civilized attitudes.

That summer the veneers fell away from Margaret and

me. We no longer had a great estate to live up to. With the departure of the blooded cattle the snob appeal was gone from Gaston Hall, for neither Margaret's lineage nor mine was a fit substitute for the royal pedigree of Bando the bull. The children did not respond to a bon mot worthy of a New York celebrity party; we soon forgot to be witty. Absorbed in the rhythmic beat of nature, we became attuned to it, shedding off little by little one artificial layer after another and rediscovering, with great pleasure, the satisfactions of a simpler life.

The genial effect of this metamorphosis tempts me to the conclusion that an absolute essential to contentment is a resolute avoidance of the temptation to be supercivilized. Too easily can happiness be killed, the innocent casualty of the war waged by the mind to impose an artificial existence against which the subconscious continuously rebels. Whether we know it or not, we yearn for the timeless fundamentals of simplicity that bring peace of mind. The heart, not the head, is ruler of us yet, and all our questing after psychiatry has not proved otherwise. Neuroses, I am inclined to believe, flourish in the veneer, not in the heart oak.

Such a philosophy would have amused me before that summer, and made Margaret scornful. Now we were no longer amused, because it had done something agreeable to us. Had this change come about in one of us, unshared by the other, the affected as well as the unaffected member might have been ashamed of it and challenged it. But it was a mutual experience, though neither of us was conscious of any change until we were separated from the environment that had produced it.

We went to New York for a few days, to renew some of our old associations. We did not have a good time. The

sophisticated pleasures, which in past years had delighted us, now left us cold. Particularly, we went to a Casadesus concert at Carnegie Hall. The soloist's technique was impeccable, but his psychological approach to the music was lost upon us. We did not appreciate his interpretations. Both of us were greatly disappointed, and I was actually shocked at my own lack of perception when Mr. Olin Downes, in the *Times*, eulogized the performance we had heard. We should have preferred, that night, the bang-bang thumping of venerable Josef Hofmann, who stomps his foot as he performs; or the firm, purposeful definitions of Myra Hess. Simplicity, to us, radiates warmth of heart.

In other ways we were confused. We had heard much of Judith Anderson's performance in the play *Medea,* which the critics rhapsodized. We found the heavy histrionics, the inflated dialogue, the stylized groupings of lesser characters, ridiculous rather than epic. The sobbings and groanings, the florid gestures, the artificial tensions, were foreign to our sympathy. We whose daily lives were free of tension did not require melodrama to divert us. I wanted to leave at the end of the first act, but Margaret, who must find out how everything turns out, insisted that we stay. We spent the second act studying the audience, and realized that our inattention was the product of our own state of mind. They all seemed carried away by the performance, which so starkly dramatized their own tensions.

The serious and frivolous distractions of the city alike antagonized us; but we had a fine time taking the children to the zoo and ferryboat riding to Staten Island, and we immensely enjoyed our reacquaintance with restaurants which offered dishes unprocurable at home. Even our conversations with friends were restricted by limitations in our point of view. We could not get excited over the frictions and problems of the city, most of which seemed to us to be the product of high tension newspaper and radio pressures. People who dwell among headlines tend to build significance out of inconsequence, crisis out of routine, and tragedy out of everything. We, who rarely read a newspaper and whose chief interest in a radio newscast is the weather report, could not work ourselves up to the required urgency of the city. We were inclined to wait until time had shrunk these daily crises to their true perspective, when we then could evaluate them in the calm atmosphere of relaxed reflection.

Recently I read an article in which a New Yorker described a reunion of his family out in Indiana. The entire clan was present, including the kissing cousins and aunts by marriage once removed. This galaxy totaled nearly one hundred persons who for a day relived the drama of their youth in staunch, Spartan Middle Western virtue. Everyone put on the dog, to convince the tribe that he had succeeded in life and was a credit to the family.

To all this hubbub the New Yorker was archly superior. He ridiculed the family traditions that day observed, and drove home in his article the thesis that intellectually the group was ovine, following like sheep the outmoded customs of its past. No chance for progress there, he concluded, and hurried back to the city thankful that he, at least, had been smart enough to shake this bourgeoise environment from his own bench-made shoes.

In reading the article, I could not escape the feeling that the writer drove his barbs too deeply, bitter that he could no longer appreciate this pumpkin pie fellowship which once had been a part of his being. Subconsciously, at least, he was nostalgic. Doubts had reared in his mind concerning his root-free life. To humble these doubts, to put his subconscious in its place, to convince himself that, divorced from his traditions he was a happy man, he lampooned the elements for which he hungered.

Traditions of some kind are a basic need of the individual, giving him nourishment from his roots, continuity of existence, and stability to offset the daily crises of urban life. They emphasize the solidarity and accentuate the consistency of family relations. More important, they feed the soul, which these days suffers from malnutrition in many people.

We returned from the city aware that our friendships henceforth must, for the most part, emerge from our new environment. This was easy to see, but difficult to accomplish, for Orange County is at once more friendly and more aloof than any other American locality I have known.

One of the oldest settlements in interior America, this section has deep roots and close family ties, which encourage clannishness. On the other hand, having been victimized during the Civil War and the Reconstruction, families hereabouts learned to live together, lest all perish, and as a result, family life is closely integrated with neighborhood welfare.

Friendliness, moreover, is inherent in the Virginian. Hospitality is a proud holdover from baronial days, when the man who owned property looked after everyone who had none. Even today, word of misfortune travels swiftly, and women will drop any activity and men leave their business establishments, to be helpful. Once when Margaret was ill, a woman she scarcely knew came over unexpectedly with a hot dinner in a basket.

History overlays every action. In olden times a man qualified as a gentleman—and wrote "Esq." after his name —if he was an Episcopal vestryman. The Episcopal standard of solidarity with timeless generations is well entrenched. Slave days bred leisure and love of pleasure, handsomeness of manners, elegant formality; these remain. The tragedies and rigors of the Civil War are close at hand, with monuments and crumbling breastworks a constant reminder of a war fought over every man's acres. After the Civil War, these people had nothing left except the land, and the determination to survive upon it under precarious economic and political circumstances. They discovered what manner of living might be extracted from the land for the enrichment of the soul. They did not allow the land to make them slaves; rather, they became masters of the land as formerly they had been masters of the Negro, and put it to work for their enjoyment.

All this reacts upon our county with contradictory effects that nonplus the foreigner and, at times, confuse the native. Yet some appreciation of the history out of which the culture has sprung is essential to the establishment of friendships here.

There is virtually no malicious gossip in these parts. The reason for this was brought home to me by a physician who, hearing me express my admiration of this trait, exclaimed, "Lord love you, lad, we can't criticize our relatives." There may be a cautionary control over gossip in an environment in which almost everyone is a kissing cousin of everyone else. Certainly one steps lightly in the drawing rooms of such family connections. But more than kinship is involved; the state of mind is charitable in this respect.

In other ways the Virginian of our county is unusual. He will drop work any time to go fishing. A New York lawyer, summoned to Orange during the war on a military contract, sent three telegrams to forecast his arrival, but his local associate did not meet his train. When finally discovered, our attorney sat with a crony on the bank of the Rapidan River, happily pursuing his avocation. The New

Yorker expostulated that he was very busy, to which the Virginian countered, "Well, so am I," and went on fishing.

There is one county resident who does not deny his wife's story that he proposed to her in the following words: "Honey, I love you, and I want to marry you. If I do, I'll do anything in the world for you except earn a living." He has lived up to his bargain and they are very happy.

There is a doctor here who is available night and day to anyone in need of medical attention. Yet he rarely sends a bill. The most common practice in settling accounts with him is to figure out once a year what is owed, then ambush the doctor as he passes the bank, hand him a check and persuade him to deposit it immediately. Otherwise, he may hold the check until he needs a new car a year or two later.

Following the Reconstruction period custom after the Civil War, the finest ladies go out at hog-killing time to render the lard, grind the sausage, salt and smoke the meat. They do this because life's enrichments come from fellowship, which in the country means the entertainment of guests. Guests must be fed. A housewife may stand for several hours watching an oven that shelters a clutch of newly hatched turkeys against a sudden damp spell, because each turkey will one day grace a buffet supper. One of the most gracious county hostesses arises every morning at half-past four to cook breakfast for seven field hands. Her action guarantees the flow of milk to market, which in turn provides the income on which her way of life depends.

The parties, which are constant, are in themselves a means to an end. Living in the country, these people have little direct access, except by books and radio, to music, the theater, and ideas. If they wish to hear music they must create it. To meet interesting people, they must invite them into their own homes. If they desire enlightenment on world affairs, they must bring the world to themselves.

This they do. One of our neighbors gives afternoon musicales. Another, whose son is a New York art dealer, entertains her son's associates. Another, formerly in the diplomatic service, has house guests from many lands. These people are shared with the entire community through the vehicle of big parties.

Under such impacts, the people keep abreast their interests. Having talked to the English sculptor Henry Moore over ham and turkey, they find their horizon for modern art extended. Having heard a concert pianist discuss a new Prokofieff sonata on a Sunday afternoon, they are aware of its nuances when later the same pianist plays it on the radio.

They never forget that the farm provender is the instrument of all this contact with the world outside. It is a medium of exchange, and glad indeed are the artists, the diplomats, the college professors, the philosophers, to exchange their ideas for a week end in the country.

Yet it is the foreigner, not the native, who properly evaluates the implications of this type of living. He observes the tenacity with which the community has preserved its existence in a turbulent world. Despite its openheartedness, the county preserves the narrow outlook and the folkways of an earlier day. Due to inadequate public education, as well as to colonial tradition, the farm owners' children are for the most part privately schooled, and receive their social, moral, political, and religious attitudes from their own homes. As a result, family solidarity is remarkable. So closely are the young people bound to the home by love and entrenched attitude that they return here in adulthood and preserve the leisurely way of life they have inherited, rather than face the complex problems of modern existence. Even after the late war, the young men came home, preferring the good life with its lack of world outlook to the current complexities of political and social change. In this respect, the community hides its head in the sands of time.

So the neighborhood is at once a paradox of openheartedness and closed-mindedness, of cultural flexibility and social rigidity, of individual charity and group intolerance.

A newcomer does not plunge into such a sea; he dips in his toes for a long time, then wades cautiously into deep water. All the time I was away in the army, Margaret was careful not to accept the casual invitations offered by well-wishers in the cashier line at Safeway, or in front of the post office.

"You must come over and see me," they'd say. Margaret registered the proper "Thank you," and that was all. Evidently these overtures had been sincere, for one day two years later, a most proper county hostess, meeting Margaret in the bank, reproached her with the words, "You haven't been to see me."

"Of course not," Margaret answered, not thinking very quickly that day. "You have not called on me."

Immediately Margaret was typed as a stickler for formality, and the word got around. People began to call. They dropped cards, properly turned down in the corner, and stayed exactly a half hour. Our callers without exception appeared to be surprised at our informality. Obviously they had expected us to be strictly tea and marmalade from four to five.

Where formerly we had allowed an hour to run to town, do our shopping, and return, such a trip now consumed the morning. Every ten steps we encountered someone to talk to. We began to understand why farmers hang around a tank town on Saturday night; the pleasure is in seeing one's neighbors. We began also to see that the question, "Where are you from?" is not, like inquiries into the weather, a casual one; it is one of the integers in a whole sum, and the addition of no man is complete without it. All our houses lean a little; friends shore up the corners and prevent the structures from falling in.

This accent on friends and family also made Margaret and me conscious of another need. With the children we had returned a call, one Sunday afternoon, on a couple who had two sons the age of our own children. En route home, Lampert asked, "Daddy, why don't we go to Sunday school?"

This was a question Margaret's mother and mine had made a careful point of avoiding, thus highlighting it by omission. The reason was quite simple. I had been reared a Methodist and Margaret a Presbyterian, and we had not yet decided in which denomination to join forces. Our new life, emphasizing the spiritual side of our existence, now brought this problem to decision. We chose the Episcopal church because it is strong in this community. But we had no idea what a complication, also motivated by the children, this affiliation would provoke. It originated in the fact that neither of the children had been baptized.

Traditionally, Episcopalian children have godparents, and nowhere is tradition more firmly seated than in Orange County. To have a baptism without sponsors would be like a wedding without witnesses: slightly questionable.

Having joined a church, Margaret and I now wanted the children baptized and enrolled in Sunday school. But godparents are chosen from lifelong friends, which of course we did not have in the community. About all we could do was to pick out a man we should be proud for our son to emulate, and a woman whose graces our daughter would do well to pattern, and hope that they would not consider us presumptuous by asking them to stand up with our off-spring.

There was no problem of selection. A cattleman who had given me much help with the farm and had gone out of his way to introduce me to other farmers had lately taken Lampert's fancy. For purposes of this narrative I shall call him Walter Harrison, a breeder of purebred Angus cattle. At a stock show he had bought Lampert a Coca-Cola, something the boy was not permitted at home, and Lampert did not forget him. Often thereafter my son inquired after Mr. Harrison's welfare and suggested we accept his invitation to go to the farm and see a horse of which Mr. Harrison had told him.

Laurie in turn was fond of another of our neighbors, who here shall be called Mrs. Prentice. She had charmed our daughter at a party she had given for her grandchildren. The charm may have been associated with a stuffed rabbit which tinkled Brahms' "Lullaby" from a music box in its stomach. By some contrivance of her own, Laurie had managed to return from the party proudly bearing this rabbit, which no doubt Mrs. Prentice had intended as a gift to one of her own granddaughters. After that, Laurie wanted to visit Mrs. Prentice every day.

These rabbit and soda water friendships were so tenuous that Margaret and I hesitated over the propriety of magni-fying them into godparentage. It was all very well for us to put the finger on these two neighbors, but how would they react to being informed suddenly that they were our very best friends, intimately connected with our family? They would be surprised, as our relationship was one of acquaintance, though a warm one. In Virginia, acquaintance is easy, friendship difficult to attain. We did not want the

simple gesture of getting the children baptized to be over-
cast with the implication that the adult Spences were attempting to entrench themselves through subterfuge.

The more Margaret and I fretted over the matter, the
more convinced we were that the prospective godparents
might decline to serve. We worried inconclusively over this
for a month, then one day at lunch decided to face the issue.

"Look," I said. "There's one way to find out—and
quietly. You put on your new dress and go over to Mary
Prentice's at teatime and ask her. Take Laurie with you, for
bait. I'll take Lampert and go to Mr. Harrison's to see that
colt. Walter will likely be in the farm office, with nobody
else around. If we get turned down, nobody will hear of it."

Margaret said she was afraid to risk it.

"That's nonsense," I rejoined. "If I have any friend in this
county, it's Walter. I certainly don't want anything un-
fortunate to happen there. But if we're going to get these
kids baptized we'd better be about it. It won't be many
years until they'll be old enough for confirmation, and I'd
sure hate to have them reach that age unbaptized. My mother
would never forgive me."

"There's plenty of time," Margaret said.

In the mail soon afterward came a letter from Mother,
saying she planned to visit us the last two weeks in August.
Since her children are scattered about now, she does not
visit us often, and I knew that nothing would make her
happier than to witness the baptism of her grandchildren.
I wrote her at once, saying that our joy at her coming would
be a double one, since the children would be baptized while
she was here. With the letter safely in the mail, I told Margaret what I had done.

Ten minutes later she brought Lampert to me, dressed
in his newest suit, his face scrubbed shiny. Margaret was

in an afternoon dress, and carried her best gloves. Laurie had on her new hat.

"All right," she said, "you take Lampert; I'll take Laurie. We're going calling. You two will have to use the truck, because I'm not going to take a thirty-five-pound daughter up to Mrs. Prentice's door in a two-ton truck."

With mutual admonitions to use unusual caution, we set out for the homes of our neighbors. Mr. Harrison seemed pleased, though surprised, at our appearance. We went to the barn and looked at the cow pony. We admired a pen of excellent bull calves. We spent some time watching the erection of a new equipment shed. Several times I almost blurted out my request, but the moment was not propitious. Later, we went to the house, joining Mrs. Harrison and her two daughters for ginger ale and cake. Lampert acted his part nobly. He was charming. He paid cavalier attention to the daughters, and shook hands with his hostess, a rare gesture for him. Suddenly I found myself back in the truck, headed for home, with the important question unasked.

The car was before the house when we returned. Margaret came out to meet us. Her face was anxious and somewhat strained.

"She got turned down," I thought.

Rather than receive this unhappy news, I told her quickly what a fine time Lampert and I had shared with the Harrisons.

"Then Walter agreed, did he?" she asked.

"No."

"He turned you down!" The shock was too much for her. She sat down on the porch step.

"Not that, either," I said. "I didn't get up courage enough to ask him."

Margaret laughed. She tried to hide her emotion, but soon her merriment was beyond concealment.

"Darling!" she said. "You're wonderful."

There have been times when I thought I was wonderful without drawing this accolade, but in this instance I saw nothing congratulatory in my actions unless . . .

Here I looked sharply at Margaret.

"You didn't ask Mrs. Prentice, either, did you?" I said.

Margaret admitted she had not. "We had a nice time," she said, "but somehow or other the time never seemed quite right."

Another week went by. An airmail letter from Mother impressed on us that her impending visit had taken on a special significance. Every line of it implied a happiness that her son and daughter-in-law had at last assumed one of parenthood's fundamental obligations. Her enthusiasm was even warmer, I think, although she did not mention it directly, over the implication inherent in this baptism that the parents of the children at last were taking some interest in the church. "I shall be proud," she wrote with that regality of faith that has always set her above most persons I have known, "to stand with you and Margaret at the altar of your church."

Now, indeed, something must be done about the godparents. I read Mother's letter to Margaret. We agreed to telephone Mrs. Prentice and Mr. Harrison that evening, but after dinner neither reminded the other, and nothing was done. The next day I called the rector and set a definite date, immediately following a Sunday service.

The day came when Mother was to arrive. Still there were no godparents. Time had run out.

"What's the matter with us?" Margaret asked.

212

"We're afraid of being thought pushy."

"If we were trying to push our way in here, we'd have been working at it the last three years, and wouldn't have this problem."

"If people would just believe that. . . ."

"I don't see how they could think otherwise."

"Then what is there to be afraid of?"

"Nothing."

Margaret gave me that peculiar, determined stare, characterized by fixed eyes and wrinkled brow, which in a family controversy implies that she has said the last word on the subject. Decisively she walked to the telephone and dialed.

"Mary?" she said next. That was Mrs. Prentice. "Laurie and I had such fun with you the other afternoon." Evidently time is relative with women, for the day of her call was now three weeks past.

A very long pause.

"Mary—I phoned you with an ulterior motive. We would like very much for you to be Laurie's godmother."

The conversation went on and on, as women's telephone talk will, but Margaret now was relaxed and smiling. At the end of the call she did not hang up the telephone. She handed it to me.

"All right," she said triumphantly. "It's your turn."

I telephoned Mr. Harrison.

"Walter," I said, "I've wanted to ask a favor of you for a month but I keep getting cold feet. How would you like to be Lampert's godfather?"

Mr. Harrison chuckled.

"What makes you think I'd qualify?"

"Lampert likes you. That's as good a reason as I can think of."

"He's quite a boy."

"I don't think he'll ever disgrace you—but if he does, he'll do it with style."

"I believe it."

"You'll take the job, then?"

There was a long pause. Then: "Why, certainly."

"That's fine."

"But don't get the wrong idea about me," he went on hurriedly. "I won't be much help to him in the matter of renouncing the devil and all his works, and I won't teach him his catechism. So on those parts of the ritual you do the promising, and I'll keep mum."

"That's all right. I just want him to have a good example."

Mr. Harrison laughed again.

"Okay," he said. "You teach him the catechism, and I'll teach him to ride, shoot, and wink at girls."

On the day of the baptism, I did not tell my mother, who stood proudly by to witness what to her must have seemed like a long-delayed event, of Mr. Harrison's role in the proceedings.

His was too much a Virginia, too much an Episcopal attitude, for Mother's Iowa Methodist convictions. At this writing, however, Lampert in his fifth year does not yet wink at girls.

CHAPTER EIGHTEEN

AROUND here, everybody talks horses. This is natural in a state which bows not to Kentucky in any aspect of horses except pari-mutuel betting. All about us are stud farms, and poor is the countryman who does not have in his stable at least one good working hunter. Three packs of hounds pursue foxes all winter within posting distance of our farm. The boundary fence between Gaston Hall and Montpelier is punctured by chicken-coop barriers. The first neighborly gesture, after we moved here, had been an invitation to join in a fox hunt. So Margaret and I were horse conscious.

But we had no riding horses. For a while this deficiency was strategic. If we were too busy to acquire and exercise mounts for the hunting season, no one would know that we rode badly. In fact, I had never been on a horse until the summer of my psychiatric confinement by the Army Air Corps. Margaret's equestrian bent was toward gaited horses which, in hunt country, are socially ostracized.

In our new freedom, however, the desire to ride grew on us. We had time to enjoy the sport. The woods about us for many miles were full of bridle trails. And we were becoming well enough acquainted that we no longer worried over what our neighbors might think of our improficiency.

One day, while the family was out looking at the yearling steers, we saw a half dozen horsemen leap the chickencoop fence between our farm and our eastern neighbor and gallop across our pasture after a pack of hounds. The victim of this excitement was a red fox, whose streaming tail we saw for a moment crossing the road toward a patch of timber.

"Boy, would I like to do that!" I said, admiring the hell-for-leather horsemanship, the eagerness of the powerful horses, the organized pandemonium of the pack of hounds.

"Why don't you, then?" Margaret inquired. The remark was quite pointed. She was having no part of it herself.

"But I can't even ride," I said.

Emphasizing our new freedom, she answered gaily, "Now's the time to learn."

And why not, I thought? After all, we had the pasture, the hay, and the oats. Little would be required except the horse, for hunting hereabouts is not a fancy sport, but a necessity to cut back the prolific population of red and grey foxes which, if unchecked, would eliminate all poultry from the countryside, and all wild game birds as well. The riders therefore are out on business and are not dressily clad. No iron hats, no pink coats, no elaborate tack.

A sound working hunter costs a lot of money. After all our talk of cutting down our establishment, I could not go out and spend on a horse the price of a three-pedestal dining-room table, which Margaret still threatened to buy. Margaret perhaps would say nothing, but she would be hurt. If given any choice, she would put the money in the dining room.

Here luck, which for two years had been a stranger to me, renewed my acquaintance. I read in the paper that the army remount depot at Front Royal, Virginia, just a few hours' drive from my gate, was liquidating its mounts at auction due to the mechanization of the cavalry. This opportunity might not come again.

Discreet inquiry revealed that the commander of the depot was away, and that the officer in charge was a major. Carefully, therefore, I donned my lieutenant colonel's uniform, so as to outrank him, and with Margaret drove to Front Royal a day ahead of the sale. I was received with the strained courtesy regular army majors usually pay to reserve lieutenant colonels. We went over the sale catalogue, eliminating the aged, the halt, the infirm, the blind, and the wind-broken. A half-dozen possibilities survived this elimination. One, a fine registered thoroughbred hunter named Trailrunner, ten years old, had formerly been General Marshall's mount when he was chief of staff. If, I reasoned, the army thought that horse safe enough for the boss, it was probably safe enough for me, because the army takes no chance of unseating five-star generals. Another, a three-gaited, half-bred nine-year-old named Soldier, seemed ideal for Margaret. Making special note of this pair, we awaited the next day's sale.

We got what we wanted, for an insignificant investment and then, carried away by the bargains, we also purchased a three-year-old thoroughbred filly of perfect conformation and little training.

The two geldings turned out to be exactly what we wanted. Within a month we sold the filly for as much as we had paid for the two geldings. I tried out the hunter on a few chicken coops and plank fences about the farm without any refusals, and several times he was ready for jumps that were too high for me. Margaret hacked the logging trails through the woods. I had a tendency to bounce overmuch, to Trailrunner's disgust. Evidently General Marshall had a better seat than I. Soldier, patient victim of many an army school and an old polo pony, had been ridden by other amateurs in his time, and was philosophical over Margaret's experiments. The horses were gentle with the children, too, when Margaret and I put them up on the saddle in front of us.

I readied myself and my mount for the hunting season with some anxiety. I was disturbed as much by ignorance of the etiquette of the hunting field as by lack of confidence. A book, however, boned me up on the deportment; hours in the saddle muscled me for the riding.

One day the master of the Montpelier hunt telephoned that he was inaugurating his season the following day and invited me along. I ducked the issue, pleading work, for frankly I was afraid, now that the time had arrived, that I might kill myself crashing through woods and meadows and over fences.

Later in the season, two neighborhood hunts combined for a New Year's Eve field. A fox, run to ground a week before, was to be turned loose, so there was no doubt of a hard ride. Both hunts invited me to participate. I could escape no longer.

The morning was cold, with a premeditation of snow. Possessing no fine riding gear, I cleaned traces of the barnyard from my field boots, donned a clean but inelegant pair of breeches, an old army shirt and a sweatshirt, a battered corduroy cap, and posted to the rendezvous. Trailrunner was clean, but he certainly was not tacked out for a horse show, and that morning he had decided to be lazy. His head drooped, and he was bored to death. My saddle was not polished. Margaret commented that I looked rather seedy for a New Year's hunt, but I reassured her. We had seen these fields going away; they were not fancy.

I was shocked when, arriving at the rendezvous, I faced

a very correct field. Sixteen beautifully conditioned horses were there, winter-clipped and neatly tacked. The riders were in their show ring best from white stock and horseshoe stickpin to shining boots. Elegant derbies and even one silk hat topped smartly cut coats. Half the county was gathered around a bonfire to speed the hunters on their way. The master wore a pink coat with a blue velvet collar; the master of hounds was gaudy in a sleek black coat resplendent with the French blue and old gold Montpelier colors in the lapels, hunting horn emblazoned across his shoulder.

Into this glitter rode I, in my laced boots, my corduroy cap, and with my disgraceful tack. Trailrunner, his ragged winter hair untrimmed, looked like a lead pony in a third-rate children's school.

"Who's that guy?" I heard someone say, and I felt like mumbling, "Oh, some field hand out rabbit hunting. Pay no attention to him."

I was introduced to the field, many of whom were strangers, resplendent names from the fashionable Keswick Hunt Club. All the dignities and amenities of a formal hunt were observed. The only thing lacking was an Episcopal bishop to bless the hounds. I wanted to go home.

But not Trailrunner. The moment he saw the hounds, he began to prance. His ears went up, his nostrils quivered, he broke like an adolescent exhibitionist into a fancy *dressage*. I dismounted quickly and went to the fire. Snow definitely was in the air now, fitful flakes motivating the hard fall that came on a few minutes later.

The fox was let out of a bag and raced into the woods. I barely had time to jump to the saddle before the hounds were away in full cry, the field crashing into the brush behind them. At least I had sense to fall in at the rear of the line.

Trailrunner, however, had other ideas. He was at home now, even though I was not. Away he went at a slow gallop, side-stepping tree trunks, washing me under low-hanging pine branches, wheeling along the turns in the trail, leaping piles of brush with champion ease. I hung on for dear life. My snaffle bit was of little use in curbing a veteran hunter who knew what he was doing and loved it.

Somewhere I lost my cap. The snow, downbeating now in fury, obliterated the path. We followed the black pock-marks of horseshoes and the enormous brown rump of the horse ahead.

The course led downward, through heavy timber. Trailrunner galloped on. Blinded by snow, knees aching, I hung on, now with my chin on the saddle to duck a low branch, now heeled down hard to jump a brook, often just along for the ride as Trailrunner, with a steady, insistent galloping gait that evidently he could maintain all day, followed the horses ahead of him. I wondered, for a fleeting second, how I had ever gotten into such company. What was I doing here? This smash through the woods was no kin to the easy gallops my horse and I had taken around the farm.

Now we came to a four-foot panel fence. Trailrunner and I had never essayed anything that high together. He went over easily. Somehow, in the snow which now was so thick that the rump ahead was no longer visible, we lost the field. We heard the hounds bay off to the right, but the crash of hoofs was gone. Immediately about us was only the gentle silence of the falling snow, the stir of a winter wind in the cedar trees.

I was not too displeased. Trailrunner turned his head impatiently and looked at me. He wanted to catch up, if I did not. We pulled off after the cry of the distant hounds, my mount pressing to overtake the others. The ride was too rough for me. I pulled up, thinking of my two children and my agreeable wife at home. Trailrunner stomped impatiently. The hounds doubled back and my mount of his own accord pursued them, breaking out of the woods beside a railroad track. Now for the first time in fifteen minutes I knew where I was. Across the track, heedless of possible trains, the horses sped. I could see that only nine remained. Somewhere in the dense woods six other hunters were lost. I felt better.

But not for long. Over a high gate we went onto the great Montpelier estate and circled the training stable. Montpelier is a horse farm, with a difficult steeplechase course for schooling race horses. The jumps are tricky, strictly for professionals. In the open land of this proving ground I saw the fox running through the snow with the hounds close behind. Crowding them was the master of the hunt, a riding demon, his derby hat sailing behind him on a string that fastened it to his collar. In file behind him were eight other riders. That one who brought up the rear, that shabby, hatless fellow who looked as though he were up on a runaway, was I.

For a mile the fox ran the steeplechase course, skirting the hurdles. The master of the hunt took every one of them, and so did that fellow in the rear. Several persons witnessed this mad chase, and reported later that the fox, the hounds, and the horses coursing over the high brush hurdles with the great mansion of James Madison in the background was a thrilling sight. I wouldn't know. Trailrunner, racing over flat, snow-slippery ground, had taken complete charge. Vainly I pulled the reins. He ignored the pressure. He was having the time of his life. Surefootedly, never interrupting for a second his beautiful gallop, he soared on and over the

221

high hurdles. There was nothing for me to do but go along.

Trailrunner was in no condition for such a hard ride. The long dash, the high barriers, the heavy going in new snow, slowed him down at last. The fox, the hounds, and the hunters outdistanced us and we pulled up behind the Montpelier greenhouse to watch the hunt race up a mountain. By the time Trailrunner was ready to resume, we had lost the field.

Now I became conscious of the fact that I was soaked with perspiration, as of course was my horse, and that the snow had yielded to a bitter wind. We headed home. After about ten minutes the hunters again came down on us, and Trailrunner was away again. I could not hold him.

A moment later the master pulled up on a knoll, from which he could watch the hounds, divided into two packs, run up parallel draws in a nearby hill. They had lost the fox.

The survivors of this epic hunt now took the first opportunity in an hour and a half of uninterrupted riding to look about and see who of the starters had had stamina enough, and horsemanship enough, to survive. And there was I.

The rest of them didn't quite believe it, but the evidence was indisputable. My horse was well-lathered, obviously hard-ridden. A crown of snow covered my head.

"I say, old man," said one of the Keswick set, expressing the common exclamation of them all, "are *you* still with us?"

The implication was clear. What he meant was, had I run the entire course? I could not, at that moment, admit having been twice lost. So I fudged a little.

I smiled, and said nothing.

CHAPTER NINETEEN

 MY preoccupation with the horses almost caused a domestic tragedy of first importance. Our old English sheep dog, Pandora, became furiously jealous.

I say she was our dog, but that is not quite accurate. By her own free choice she belonged to me, and to me alone.

I remember the day she came into my life. I was in the Air Corps hospital and the psychiatrist, in his omniscience, decided that I needed a puppy to love and care for. What motivated his conclusion I do not know. He had been psychoanalyzing the dog, who had her own peculiar problem, had decided that what she required was a great deal of loving attention, and there I was, with nothing to do.

My suspicion that Pandora came to me for her good, rather than for mine, emerges from the detailed diagnosis of her condition that accompanied her presentation. She had a chronic car sickness, the psychiatrist said. With her mother, a champion, she had been en route by automobile to a benching show when only a few days old. The car had struck another and overturned. Since then, though Pandora loved to ride, to do so made her ill. Particularly the sound of an auto horn upset her. But it was nothing, the psychiatrist informed me with authority, that love and patience could not cure.

This psychiatrist, a long-legged, shy young introvert, had also discovered, in his remorseless probing of my antecedents, that never in my life had I owned a dog, or cared to own one. This, to him, was significant. A great bird-dog man himself, he could not understand that anyone capable of free choice would exist without a canine companion high in his quota of affections. Without a positive lust for a dog pet I was, to his mind, abnormal. Having determined my abnormality, which no doubt in psychiatric terms would be labeled a caniphobia, he prescribed for me the care and feeding of one dog.

In private life one may reject the diagnosis of a physician and seek more compatible medical counsel. In the army, however, not even a general officer may dispute the wisdom of the medical department.

There is something nobly rollicking in the military thought process, that it will team a greying lieutenant colonel and a three-month-old puppy, both of whom have pyschiatric aberrations. The whole thing was done without any hint of a sense of humor. Papers were written in triplicate concerning it, orders cut and stencilled, and a request conveyed, over the commandant's signature, for the Red Cross to yield to me one puppy then under its jurisdiction. The end result of this humorless process was an order to me to report to headquarters, where I was given formal custody of the most forlorn little mass of tangled hair that had ever been untimely ripped from the ministrations of its natural mother.

Pandora was the daughter of a famous old English sheep dog of the Pantaloons strain. She had been donated to the Red Cross, for the worthy cause of rehabilitation, by the kennel of her origins. She was a Greek gift: for she did not, even at that tender age, convey those characteristics of the breed that are lauded in the benching shows. Rather she was something out of Thurber, with an overgrown, forlorn head and tragic big black eyes, a gaunt, dumpy figure crowned by an enormous rump, legs too thin for her length, and pads much too small to counterbalance the big head. Her coat, which even in the puppy sheep dog is dense, was notably thin, particularly at the brow and down the center of the back. Never did she display the good-humored puckishness of puppyhood. From the beginning she was a staid and dignified lady, contemptuous of other dogs and haughty toward every human. Every human, that is, except one. She adored me.

The adoration was not mutual. I accepted her belligerently, publicly acknowledging that on the day the army, in its wisdom, transferred me from this hospital, Pandora and I were quits, or sooner if the psychiatrist permitted. Since I was under orders to care for the beast, I would do so. I cleaned her up and took her to my quarters.

A captain who sojourned in the cottage next to mine had had under his care for some weeks an Afghan hound to whom he was much attached. Without complaint or even a ruffle of temper he had policed his rooms of the hound's carelessness, and had spent hours on the lawn, an instruction book in one hand, a brush in the other, grooming and training his canine friend. I had watched these antics with some disdain. Grown men, it seemed to me, should have more constructive intellectual enthusiasms than puppies, and certainly less patience over befouled lodgings. The captain was not at all abashed by my attitude. He loved that hound, though the Afghan quite obviously would have preferred almost any other company to his, and showed no inclination, even after weeks of repetitious training, to heed his master.

The captain was on the lawn when I approached, my puppy trailing happily at my heels. He could see my shame and, like all good dog lovers, he reveled in it.

"Now you will get to know man's best friend," he said. "And you will no longer tell me, my fine colonel, that the monuments to these noble animals which man from time to time has carved in words are mere saccharine sentimentalities." He was a stuffy sort of fellow, the captain, which may have been one reason the Afghan didn't like him.

"Come on, Pandy," I said. The lady came immediately to heel.

The captain was surprised. His Afghan, for all his training, would not do that.

"I say!" the captain exclaimed, alive with interest now in Pandy herself. He fancied himself somewhat on his eye for dogs, and had done a bit of judging, the week before, at a Vassar College show at Poughkeepsie. With professional appraisal he eyed my pup, and he was visibly disturbed. He rubbed her head, held up her chin to look in her mouth, felt her nose, and rubbed a speculative finger along her coat.

"She's nice," he said, politely and without enthusiasm, "but what is she supposed to be?"

"An English sheep dog," I said.

"An *old* English sheep dog?"

"Three months old," I said.

"I know, I know. But the breed, sir. Old English sheep dog is a breed. You must be mistaken."

"Oh, no," I said. "Here's the pedigree right here."

"Pedigree!" This was beyond belief. He took the paper in his hands as though it was an unclean thing, and read it. Several times, after glancing at illustrious names which apparently were familiar to his eye, he looked at Pandora, as though attempting to discover some genetic resemblance.

226

"Where did you get her?" he asked at last.

"Red Cross."

He nodded. In Italy, his lungs a sieve of shrapnel punctures, he had been denied cigarettes at a base hospital and had begged a Red Cross girl for half a day to break the rule and put a lighted cigarette in his war-torn mouth. She had, of course, refused. Since that day he had hated the Red Cross.

Pandy and I left him. Or rather, I left him and Pandora, ignoring the sniffing friendliness of the Afghan, turned and followed me.

I sat on my bed and thought what I should do next. Pandy cuddled into a warm ball against my shoes. Nothing seemed to be required of me, so I did nothing. Careful not to disturb her, I reached for a book, and in that manner the morning passed. If by chance I moved my foot an inch or two, Pandora uncurled herself, edged forward until she touched me again, and resumed her slumbers.

At lunchtime I was perplexed as to whether to leave my charge in my quarters or not. She settled the matter for me. She trotted beside me to the messhall and, crawling under the table, again curled up at my feet. The afternoon was a continuous struggle between my feet, to rid themselves of her, and her determination not to be disconnected. There was only a moment of refuge. About four o'clock I went swimming. She would not go in the water. Her eyes did not leave me, even when I swam to the diving raft. She trailed along the shore, keeping as close to me as the water would allow, yet did not set a pad in the water.

I made no attempt to train her. Never once did she abuse my quarters. She slept on a small cotton rug beside my shoes at night and, except when she was tied up, followed me everywhere. She began to grow, in the most incongruous way, accentuating the big head, the sad eyes, and lean figure, her torso seeming even more slender because of the thinness of the hair upon her back.

From the beginning, I had only to say sharply, "Pandy!" and she would leave off whatever displeased me. One day, departing for the recreational hall where dogs were not allowed, I barked "Pandy!" when she attempted to follow me. She stopped. "Go home!" I said, and pointed.

She knew perfectly well what I meant. Her black eyes became even more sorrowful and her head went slowly down until her chin was almost on the ground.

"Go home!" I repeated. The captain came to his door to watch this clash of wills. He had often ordered his Afghan to remain home, only to find, ten miles down the road, that the hound was running behind his car.

Pandy's whole body drooped, as though she had been cruelly whipped. She looked up longingly, begging me to rescind my order. I could not stare her down. I turned and began to walk. Not hearing her behind me, I walked faster. After ten yards of this, I heard behind me the captain's voice, quietly saying, "Bravo. Good dog." I looked back. Pandy was lying forlornly just outside the door of my quarters, her eyes still upon me.

"Good dog," I said. Her rear end wiggled violently.

This was too much.

"All right," I said. "Come on."

Pandy was beside me in a moment. Now I could not go to the recreational hall, so I changed direction and headed for the tennis court. Behind me, in a voice at once sarcastic and gloating, I heard the captain say, "Good man."

One cannot live upon such adoration without being affected by it. When I left the hospital Pandy, of course, was with me. She was maturing now, a nine-month-old, and plainly evident was the fact that she would never be a beauty, or a compliment to her breed. She looked, in body, something like the pictures of old-style working sheep dogs before they went fancy and grew hair so long they couldn't see, except for the largish head with its deep-seated brooding eyes, and the feet ridiculously small for her over-all dimensions. By that time I did not care at all what she looked like. She was my dog.

We came home from the war together, and she loved the farm at once. However untrue to her breeding she may have been in conformation, she was true to it in deeds. She understood instinctively how to round up the cattle and would circle, without being told, to drive the cattle through a gate, but always in such a manner that her eyes were always on me, awaiting my signal. In this way she saved me many steps, and the cattle came to know and fear her until, at the sight of her, they would walk toward the open gate.

Everywhere I went, she was with me. If she was in the house, in somnolent composure on the hall carpet, and I so much as put a hand on my hat, she bolted immediately to the door. If she was outside and I was inside, she could always be found under a tree seat in the back yard, her eyes on the door through which eventually I would pass. No matter what I asked her to do, she obeyed implicitly.

Once romping in a field with the dog I thought I saw a new calf beside its dam far over the hill along a creek. I began to walk in that direction. So great was the agitation of the cow at Pandy's approach that I was afraid she might do her newborn babe an injury. I therefore pointed to the ground and said to Pandy, "Lie down." She was down at once. I examined the new calf, then began a general inspection of the herd which lasted some time. This completed, I returned to the house. More than an hour later I remembered that I had left Pandy on the hillside. As I returned then to the hill, she saw me from afar off. I did not signal her for I did not want her to know I had forgotten her. Instead, I walked to her, patted her on the head, rubbed her coat, and paid her the most extravagant attention. I said, "All right, girl, let's go home." She ran joyously ahead of me.

On another occasion, during a dinner party, the subject of canine obedience arose, and I mentioned that my Pandora was not allowed in the living room because she would soon ruin the light carpet, but that if I invited her in, and then asked her to leave, she would do so without being told twice. My dog-loving friends were skeptical of this.

"Pandy," I called softly. She raised her head. Always, when I was in the living room, she lay just outside the door.

"Come here, girl."

She hesitated. She had never been invited into the living room before and she did not understand this unwonted indulgence. Slowly, her whole body plainly indicating that this whim was mine rather than hers, she came to me. She did not, as in the library, curl up immediately into a ball at my feet, inviting me to stroke her back with my shoe, which she dearly loved. She just stood there.

"These folks don't think you'll obey me," I said. "But you will, won't you?" Her pink, moist tongue obtruded from her mouth, and she flipped her head, a signal that she wanted her ears scratched. I obliged. I gave her a thorough scratching. When even she had had enough, I said, still quietly, "All right, Pandy. That's all. Leave the room."

She was crushed. The black eyes were infinitely mournful. Her body shrank, her mouth closed. Nervously once she licked her nose and alternately raised each front paw in protest. When I said nothing more, she shambled from the room and lay down again in the doorway. I could not look at her long. As plainly as though she had said the words she conveyed to me the message, "That was a dirty trick."

When I had brought Pandy home, I thought she might become a companion to the children, then both babies. She took no interest in them. Tolerantly she let Lampert and Laurie tug at her whiskers and climb on her back. If they became too rough, she nipped them on the wrist, accompanying the gesture with a frightening growl. Examining the children's arms, however, I never found any trace of lacerations.

Pandy did not take to Margaret, either. If Margaret gave Pandy a command, the dog ignored it. Yet Margaret had only to invoke my assistance by mentioning my name, and Pandy would obey before I intervened. Clearly she had understood Margaret's words all the while.

At the proper season we decided that Pandy required fulfillment. Several neighborhood mongrels were also of this notion. My publisher owned a fine bench-type sheep dog of patrician birth and champion points, named Neville. Somewhat a notable among dogs, Neville had traveled from England on the maiden voyage of the steamship *Normandie*. Luckily, my publisher had planned an extended trip and did not wish to leave his dog in a kennel. We undertook to board Neville for his services.

Pandy liked him well enough, for he had that strong, silent mien and virile physique which the female sex loves. He was enormous, his pads making mud stains four inches in diameter on our rugs. Hair completely covered his face, obliterating his eyes. His coat was so thick that in one sprint through the timber he would pick up two hundred wood ticks. He was a real gentleman. Quickly he learned how to open the screen door by butting it with his head and catching it with his nose as it rebounded, so he had access to the house at any time. He observed, however, that Pandy could not master this trick, and from then on he held open the door for her before he entered. Both dogs were barred from the living room because of the pink rug there. After dinner, Neville would lie down just outside the door, his nose on the sill. In a moment or two he would shift his haunches, moving his body forward about an inch. In fifteen minutes he was inside the room and had to be sent out, to make a new start. Pandy admired this performance, though her own discipline was too strong to permit her to emulate it. With growing agitation she would watch his ambulant progression until he received his order to retire, at which she would invariably open wide her mouth as though giving him a horse laugh.

On Neville's arrival, Pandy watched me carefully for a day, and was gratified to see that I paid him no particular heed. Thus reassured, she acquainted him with her favorite haunts about the farm, the best places in which to flush rabbits and chase squirrels and filch grain. Early each morning she took him on a tour of our end of the county, begging at every kitchen door, for Neville's appetite was insatiable. Neville understood why he was visiting in Virginia, and tried his best to be an obliging guest. Pandy repulsed him archly, as befitted a lady whose heart was given elsewhere.

We concluded finally that since Pandy was abnormal physically she was also barren, and shipped Neville home. From that moment we let her run. Two years later Laurie, who liked to stroke Pandy when the dog lay asleep with her four feet straight up in the air, commented that our Pandy seemed to have grown some underneath. Pandy was almost to term.

The next day six puppies were born, sired evidently by

one of the Montpelier beagle hounds. Pandy never was much of a mother. She would leave her whelps the moment I emerged from the house, and range the fields with me even when her cups were overflowing.

When the horses arrived, Pandy was on hand to greet them. As usual, she was suspicious of any innovation in which I expressed an interest, and as I began to spend many hours with Trailrunner, Pandy turned sulky. Several times, in a jealous pique, she overtook the gelding in pasture and nipped his flanks. In consequence, Trailrunner was skittish when Pandy accompanied us on our rides, and I had to leave her at home. There were two hurdles in the woods over which I exercised the horse. Barred from the scene, Pandy craftily edged up through the underbrush until she knew that one more inch would expose her to the horse. Putting her head between her paws at this point, she watched until the exercise ended, then sneaked back to the house to greet me innocently on my return.

With the arrival of the hunting season, Pandy's problem became more complex. She could find no vantage point from which to observe us, since we ranged over many miles, and she was compelled to remain at home. This she could not understand. For three years she had been my incessant companion, and now she had lost me to a horse.

She brooded over this. At first she met me, on my return from hunting, with boisterous affection designed to rewin my exclusive attention. I was careful to respond to these overtures with avowals of constancy. In a few days, however, she no longer believed my words, and watched me set out on a hunt, from her vantage under the tree seat, without even a wag of her tail. Likewise, she ignored me on my return. If I went to her and ruffled the thin hair atop her head, a gesture that formerly had produced ecstacies of joy in her, she looked up reproachfully, without moving. She went to the house for her food on heavy feet.

The day came when she did not come to the house at all. On days when I did not ride, she refused my companionship. Lethargic and woebegone, she remained motionless for hours. No artifice would entice her from beneath the tree seat. She had been jilted; she wanted none of me on a part-time basis.

Within a week her incongruous body was shrunken and dehydrated. The thin hairs on her back fell out. She spurned such offerings as a beef bone filled with marrow. Clearly she had developed a will to die.

I had been planning a business trip, but postponed it, hoping to revitalize her. I stopped riding; she chose not to notice. I consulted the veterinarian about forced feeding, which he advised against. Glee thought Pandy was so far gone that she should be destroyed, and knowing how I felt, proposed that he dispose of her.

Days wasted away, and Pandy with them. Every night before I retired I went to her. She rebuffed me coldly. After the house lights were out, she wobbled to her feet, stumbled to a stream below the house, drank slowly for a long time, and returned to the tree seat for the night.

One morning the blacksmith who came each month to shoe the horses telephoned that he had been hurt and could not make his usual visit. Soldier and Trailrunner were both in need of attention, so Glee decided to post five miles into the mountains to a blacksmith shop.

I watched from behind the house as Glee, up on Trailrunner and leading Soldier, set out down the road. He was anxious as to whether Soldier would allow himself to be led. At the gate he turned and waved, signalling assurance. I returned his gesture. The horses disappeared behind a knoll. At that moment I felt a familiar muzzle at my knee. Pandy was beside me. She looked up most gratefully, licked her nose and stood, mouth open and panting, ready to obey me again. I took her to the house and fed her, after which she shambled to her accustomed place on the hall rug.

Later, taking the car, I overtook Glee up the mountain road, to be sure he was not in trouble. Pandy, of course, was with me. She had never quite outgrown her car sickness, and fretted a good deal at every ride, but she would not be left at home. When we passed the horses on the road, Pandy thrust her head far out the car window and leered. We went home by a different road.

Pandy, nothing but bones and a big head with black eyes set in it, was satisfied at last. She slobbered her wet tongue over my ears in her first demonstration of affection in many days. Now I was really in trouble, for Pandy was sure that the horses had left the farm. Late that afternoon I headed off Glee as he was returning, and put the horses in a rented pasture some miles away. There they remained for a month, while Pandy fattened and forgave me.

The hunting season had ended before the horses were brought home. Pandy saw them approach before I did. She came to me, stepping nervously on alternate front feet and thrusting her head from side to side. I gave Trailrunner a lump of sugar as the horses passed the house and then walked, with Pandy at my heels, to the pasture gate. The horses were turned out and fled at once across a hill. As we watched them go, I kept my hand on Pandy's head, scratching deeply into her fur.

She never sulked again.

CHAPTER TWENTY

OCCUPATION with dogs and horses and children was a pleasant holiday after four years of turmoil. For several months we coasted along, enjoying life, and developing a resistance toward hard work without any suspicion that this idyl was about to come to an abrupt end.

I would nod casually toward the front lawn and say, "Look at that grass. I simply must cut it tomorrow."

"Certainly," Margaret would reply. She knew I had no intention of mowing the lawn until the weeds threatened to seed. I had ceased to be the slave of a greensward, just as Margaret had stopped being the drudge of a household. By common consent we did not needle each other about these shortcomings. I might mention the uncut grass but she did not, just as she might exclaim about the cobweb that had been for three days on the hall ceiling, though I ignored it. Meticulousness as to details became unimportant; somehow the deliberate avoidance of annoyance became important.

About that time a sewing bag was hung behind the door of our bedroom. It was part of our new state of mind. All my married life I had lived in the excitement of never knowing, when I took a clean shirt from a drawer, whether there would be buttons on it or not. My socks had a tendency toward undarned holes. Ripped garments were likely to stay ripped. For several years I commented on these annoyances, but without success. The best way not to get a button sewed was to mention the need of it. Sooner or later, usually much later, Margaret in a fit of industry would spend an entire day with her needle and repair everything in sight, not only my clothes and those of the children, but also the draperies, rugs, towels, bed linen, and her own wardrobe.

One day, during an interval of disrepair, I lost my temper and addressed certain words to no one in particular concerning the virtues of a domesticated woman. As is always the case with a wife, Margaret took this remark personally.

"You mean," she intervened, popping her head suddenly in the door, "that I should sit down and sew on buttons as fast as they pop off; is that it?"

"No," I replied, backtracking rapidly, "I just don't like to put my hand in a dresser drawer full of allegedly wearable clothes and come up with something like this." For illustration, I held aloft several pairs of socks, each containing a hole either in one heel or the other. "It isn't systematic," I explained.

"All right," Margaret said. "You are not objecting to the holes, then, or the lack of a button—just the lack of system."

"That's right."

The next day the sewing bag was installed behind the door. All unmended clothing went in the bag. No longer do I find any offense in the bureau—I find no shirts and socks at all. They are in the mending bag. This, to Margaret, is an effective compromise.

Our attitude toward our trees changed, too. The house is surrounded by them, all tall, expansive, and beautiful. Coming as we do from the Middle Western plains where

237

trees are scarce, we have a great respect for them and for a long time would not cut one even for practical purposes.

A certain gum tree, however, was an annoyance to me. I was well aware of its symmetry, for it stood on the front lawn exactly between the front porch and the mountains. One evening, while craning my neck around the gum's dense foliage for a glimpse of the sunset, I remarked, "Margaret, if that one tree were cut, we could see the mountains much better."

"Oh, we can't cut that," Margaret said.

"Why not?"

"Well—there are a lot of people who wouldn't like it, for one thing."

"They don't have to live with it," I said. "It seems idiotic to preserve a tree that blocks our entire view. If it were the only tree on the farm, it would be different."

"It's the only gum tree."

I stopped talking then, which was probably a good idea, because I began to think. I concluded that a propaganda campaign might do, with subtlety, what direct complaint would not accomplish.

A few days later, returning to the farm from the home of a neighbor along a road from which our house was visible, I stopped the car.

"You know," I said, "the house seems lopsided from here. I wonder what causes it?" I drove on.

A few days later I suggested that we have a picnic on the lawn. I chose the site with care, just north of the gum tree, before which the entire vista of the Blue Ridge was spread out as though part of our yard. Fortunately the evening was ideal, with a beautiful sunset. At the proper moment, I adjourned the picnic and we retired to the porch for a

238

last glimpse of the solar fireworks. The sunset could not be seen. The gum tree was directly in the way.

The next day Margaret inquired concerning the cost of cutting it down. I protested that it would be too heavy right now. Maybe next year.

"But you are the one who wanted it out!" she exclaimed.

"I know," I said, "but I've been reading up on gum trees. They are very hard to exterminate. New shoots come up from the old roots as soon as the trunk is gone. Besides, it would leave an ugly stump."

"Nonsense," Margaret said. "A stick of dynamite would fix that."

"Not a gum stump," I said. "Those things pull hard. The grain runs every which way, so they won't crack up, and you can't even drive a wedge into them. It can't be done."

A few days later I went to New York. Margaret met the train on which I returned. There was a significant sparkle in her eyes, as when she is about to prove to me that she can make a pinafore for Laurie out of an old army shirt, dyed red. She did not take me directly home. Instead, we drove to the stretch of road from which our house is visible in its nest of meadows.

"What do you think?" she asked, stopping the car.

The house was clearly visible, all one hundred fifty feet of it.

"Looks great," I said. "What did you do?"

She drove home without replying. The gum tree was gone from the lawn. Even the brush had been hauled away. Only an ugly stump remained, and I noticed as we drove rapidly by it at dangerous speed that it was mightily charred, as though someone had spent a lot of time trying to burn it. Margaret stopped before the porch.

239

"Now look at the view," she said. The Ridge, deeply blue as after a thundershower, was exposed for its entire eloquent length.

"It's wonderful," I said.

"Don't tell me," Margaret said, "that something can't be done."

Instinct told me that this was not the time to mention the unsightly stump. In fact, it is still there.

We also developed a new point of view concerning the swimming pool. At first this ostentatious structure, with its two bathhouses, excited us. We never got round to repairing the pool, however, and finally we no longer wanted to restore it, for it implied an economic level that we could not and did not desire to live up to. There is no such connotation, either to outsiders or to ourselves, in an ornate swimming plant gone derelict. Lately we have even been considering putting the pool to economic use as a breeding ground for Muscovy ducks.

On the farm, meanwhile, the reorganization was complete. We had converted our one hundred sixty acres to pasture and hay and were feeding steers. We bought the young stock and turned it out to grow. Except for a few days of haying in summer, and an hour a day of feeding in winter, the cattle required little attention and Glee, now our only permanent employee, devoted most of his time to maintenance and repair. With this low overhead, the farm gave indications, in that fifth summer of our rural life, of paying its own way at last.

We had looked forward happily to midsummer when, for the first time, we should have time to enjoy the many guests from the city who drop in on us. The first of these were two little girls from Brooklyn. They were sent by a fresh air fund, whose solicitor had convinced us that we should give these children of the city streets a fortnight sample of a way of life different in conduct, speech, attitude, and environment from their own. Presumably they were to gain something from this experience.

By social service standards the girls were underprivileged. Brownie, a shy eleven-year-old with frightened brown eyes and a tendency to tears, had never before been away from her native city. Her mother left home before dawn to work in a pickle factory; her father was an invalid. Brownie was a healthy child, deeply religious, sensitive both in complexion and spirit, stub-nosed, curly of hair, definitely Irish in antecedents.

Angela was a well-muscled, illiterate ten-year-old with a loud voice, vigorous manner, and affectionate nature, and definitely no angel. She had completed four years of schooling but could not spell her own Italian name, or read the letters she received almost daily from her mother. I gathered, from these epistles packed with admonitions to good behavior, that at home Angela was something of a tomboy. Worldly-wise and cynical, moonfaced and boisterous, Angela arrived with a shaven head. She had been shorn at the railroad station by the fresh air fund officials to rid her of certain objectionable traveling companions. At home she went bowling with her uncle on Saturday nights while her father and twenty-year-old brother, both laborers, entertained Angela's mother and elder sister, and evidently a goodly census of the neighborhood, over a bottle of Chianti.

Brownie and Angela explored the entire farm during the first hour of their arrival, while our own two children raced

241

along on tiny feet fruitlessly attempting to follow. The girls were not impressed by their inspection. Quite the reverse. They turned our establishment into a suburb of their own experience in very short order, and from then on for two weeks we all were living in Brooklyn.

The girls declined the amusements of our own youngsters, drawing scathing parallels between the underprivileged life of our children, who had only daisy fields to roam and haymows to jump in, and the Brooklyn of elaborate playground equipment in the parks, roller coasters at the beaches, and lovers "smoosing" behind shadeless windows. Even a swimming pool was too dignified for them; they preferred a hose in our back yard, for this was akin to the rough and tumble of a fire hydrant splashing forcefully across a paved street. Of all they saw, only the horses impressed them. Of all they did, the high light was a trip to town to the dime store and the movies.

Both the girls were Catholics, and I took them to confession on Saturday night, since both desired to receive the communion at church the following day. Father Castillon and I were old friends. After ministering to the girls he emerged from the church quite perplexed and asked searching questions concerning their background while Angela and Brownie remained inside. Evidently the good father, a Belgian missionary priest, had never before encountered the like of these children, and was hard pressed to understand them. He kept blinking his eyes studiously and rubbing his hand over a rutted brow.

The girls gave him little time for these researches, however. They raced from the church, piled into the car, and waved jauntily to the priest as we headed for home. Then they became silent. This was phenomenal, since Angela had been continuously vocal since her arrival. Obviously the girls were settling something in their minds. It was Angela, of course, who spoke first.

"What penance did he give you?" she asked.

"Three Hail Marys," Brownie responded.

"Me, too," Angela snorted. "Boy, boy! I'd never get off that light at home."

She was disappointed. The discipline of her own priest, who undoubtedly knew her quite well, was more realistic.

By now we were driving up Main Street, which though not large, has its points, particularly in the way of antebellum buildings. Again Angela broke the silence, swiping wide her arms to include the town.

"What a dump!" she shouted. "One dime store, one movie, and three Hail Marys. Leave me get back to civilization!"

Our children, of course, loved Angela and Brownie, padding the farm after them constantly, or sitting quietly as young rabbits while, with wide eyes they absorbed the Brooklyn speech and attitudes. Undone in a fortnight was a year of careful training. Long after the departure of our guests, Laurie would climb on my lap, slobber me with wet kisses, and say, "Ah, come on, pop, let's do a little smoosing."

Whatever impression the girls received of us, they certainly left one with us. For two weeks we were in the midst of the city, its problems, its hopes for a better future, its battle against the bafflements of a highly complex civilization; and above all, its vitality. We were pepped up. We were also disturbed. For we, who had invited these children from a sense of duty and were therefore ready to patronize them, had instead been patronized by them.

Not long after this episode, a theatrical impresario I had known in the army happened to be in Washington and telephoned to us. We invited him to the farm, and he was delighted. He needed a rest, he said. This I did not doubt, for Basil works harder than anyone I know. His days are a fever of interviews, haggles over contracts, and collisions with temperamental personalities; his nights are a round of parties and clubs and benefits at which he must be seen to maintain his standing in the profession. For years he has borne this schedule, collapsing into bed at four in the morning, at his desk again before noon. If he leaves this grind, it is to fly to Hollywood and back so rapidly that his absence from New York will not be noticed.

Basil appeared for breakfast the morning after his arrival in smart country clothes, complete to blue suede shoes and a silk scarf under a Deauville sports shirt. His pleated trousers were elegantly pressed. I told him I had about an hour of work to do on the farm, and he expressed a desire to accompany me on my rounds. We walked through a little mud getting to a hilltop from which I could count the steers and check them against signs of illness. He trod delicately through a wallow while I roused a brood sow and herded her to the maternity yard. He watched with polite interest while I replaced a stable door that had blown from its hinges in a recent wind, then eyed me with critical distaste as, fork in hand, I pitched the bedding from the stable floor into a manure spreader and put down new straw.

"Just one more little chore," I said, heading toward the house. "Want to help?"

"Sure," Basil said.

I had noticed an eave trough on the house that leaked a little, and brought up an extension ladder to repair it. All Basil had to do was to stand on the edge of the roof, pull up on a rope a twenty-five-pound can of cement, and hold it for me. He could not do it. After two minutes on the roof he complained of dizziness and went below, where he took a bunch of grass and carefully cleaned his shoes. When I came down, my work done in ten minutes, he was looking out across the valley to the Blue Ridge, which that day was deep in azure.

"How repulsive!" he exclaimed with frank distaste. "What a way to live!"

We had scarcely put Basil on the train when we received a telegram heralding the visit of another old friend, Ned Sears. Ned is an important magazine editor, one of the few friendships I made in college which has survived the years. Both Margaret and I were extremely fond of him. We had not seen him, however, since before the war, and during this interval he had risen from a newspaper desk to his present eminence. I had heard that he had put on the dog lately, and lived in an elaborate penthouse, which seemed odd to me, for he made his reputation as a left-winger.

Since we expected Ned to radiate a penthouse personality, we decided to impress him a little with our own way of life. There was an ulterior purpose here, too, for I thought I might sell him an article for his magazine about our county and its people.

Before we went to town to meet Ned's train, Margaret spent considerable time at her dressing table, and donned her best tweedy suit. Ned, a bachelor, had always been an admirer of smartness in the feminine sex.

"I guess you'll impress him, all right," I said as Margaret came downstairs to where I stood, watch in hand, waiting. "You even impress me."

"I don't have a chance to dress up very often," Margaret laughed. She went to the kitchen to impress some last-minute instructions on a girl we had hired to cook and serve the dinner. Then, as women will when they are already late,

Margaret thought of something else and rushed to the dining room, where she took down some demitasses dusty from long disuse and carried them to the kitchen to be washed. To me, this meant that, carried away by my compliment, she had decided to wear a dinner dress that night, which called for coffee in the living room.

That afternoon we drove Ned about the countryside, showing him some of the seventy-two antebellum houses and giving him the flavor of the community. He asked searching questions and I, revising upward the fee I would ask for my article, embellished the actual facts a bit to pique his editorial interest.

My enthusiasm was short-lived, however. After dinner, over which Margaret presided in a gold dress which revealed little ankle but much shoulder, we retired to the living room for our coffee. Ned spurned the demitasse.

"How about giving me a man-sized cup of coffee, with cream and sugar?" he asked. Margaret summoned our maid-for-the-evening and the request was gratified.

"Thank you," Ned said. He took a deep swallow, then looked at me challengingly and pointed to the coffee tray.

"Did you ever stop to consider," he said, "that life around here is very much like that little bone china cup?"

"In what way?" I asked.

"It has no relation to actuality before eight o'clock at night—and even then only a limited reference."

Margaret, who until that moment had enjoyed her role of elegant hostess, paused in the act of pouring her own coffee.

"You don't really mean that, Ned," she said.

"Oh, but I do," our guest replied quickly. He held up his own cup. "A man can get a drink out of this. It is big, it is satisfying, and nourishing—as life should be. But this—" he picked up a demitasse from the tray, "what is it? A pretty little refinement. It has a certain amount of elegance, but offers nothing substantial."

"And neither do we. Is that what you mean?" Margaret asked. She interprets every argument personally.

"I do," Ned agreed seriously. "Forgive me for saying so, but in this demitasse I see your county quite clearly. It is fragile and" he paused as though editing copy with a punctuation mark, "—antique."

That Margaret and I had given Ned this impression during the afternoon occurred to me, and perhaps to Margaret, too, for she now hurried to dispel the misunderstanding.

"I don't think you quite appreciate . . ."

"Oh, but I do," Ned cut her off. "All day you have been showing off the neighborhood. Obviously you are both proud of it. To me it is a vestigial tail of the feudal system, still wagging for the privileged few. You yourselves have also become demitasse—only half a cup."

My impulse was to deflate his figure of speech by pointing out that the cups had been used only three times in four years, but the discussion was interesting, so I extended it.

"Must one drink from an unbreakable cafeteria mug in order to live?" I asked.

"It helps," Ned said. "The mug and the working man go together. Both clumsy and both indestructible. Life has no meaning except in terms of achievement, which means work. What can you possibly achieve in this environment?"

"What's wrong with our environment?" Margaret asked. She was beginning to get personal again.

"Why, you've gone to seed!" Ned exclaimed.

Margaret rose and took her coffee to the fireplace, over which hung a large mirror. I saw her quickly appraise herself for tokens of seediness. One hand nervously rubbed a line from her forehead. Prudently I ended the discussion by summoning the children from the library. That, of course, stopped all talk for a while.

Margaret did not shake off Ned's visit lightly. She said nothing at all to me, but for several days she paused, every time she passed a mirror, and subjected her face to studious appraisal. Then one morning she returned from town with a book which absorbed her for a day and an evening. I knew it was having an extraordinary effect on her, because she devoted to it an intense, exclusive concentration. Lunch was a half-hour late, despite the fact that the maid-for-an-evening we had hired to impress Ned had stayed on as a permanent cook. Margaret would not go to the table until she had completed a chapter. A list of a dozen chores she had intended to do lay ignored upon her desk. The children devoted to me the most flattering attentions, indicating thus that they were getting none from their mother.

A jar of skin cream lay on a table beside her, and from time to time she absently dipped into it with her finger tips and rubbed her face. A long scab of Scotch tape was stretched across her brow.

That evening I attempted to discover the nature of Margaret's book, but she reads with the volume in her lap, and I could not see the title. Once she left the room to answer the telephone and I leaped to examine her opus, to discover that she had taken it with her.

During all this diligence she did not mention the subject of her deep study. I knew it was not a romance, for Margaret gulps novels, scanning the complications superficially in a furious race to the denouement. This omnivorousness is retarded only when some lurid passage suggests a good cry, in which case she enjoys it utterly before surging forward again. I knew also that her book was not a biography, because obviously she was going to read it to the last page. It was not a critique on art or interior decoration or a handbook on how to bring up children, for she had no interlineating pencil in her hand. It definitely was not a mystery tale because she did not, from time to time, give me the benefit of her own clairvoyant deductions. No, this was something big, something new, something far afield from her usual tastes.

Long after bedtime I remained downstairs, having exhausted my own book and magazine and undertaken a game of solitaire to pass away the time. Suddenly she leaped up, her eyes glowing, and exclaimed, "I'm a new woman!"

At that moment I saw the title of the book. It was *How Not To Be Tired*. I suggested that weariness was best counteracted by retiring at a reasonable hour, but this irony was lost on her. She stood, her fingers interlaced behind her neck, and without even yawning said, "This book has something." With that she dropped it into a chair and swept off to bed in a studious fog.

The next day Margaret was awake and gone before I arose. My first act, of course, was to scrutinize the book that threatened once more to disturb the serenity of our ways. Evaluating it in terms of Margaret, I could see its appeal to her. Living an isolated life in the country she did lack stimulating interests. Her fatigue was mental. To be witty, gay, and strong as a horse, a woman needs some program, the book said, that would take her outside herself.

Margaret returned, late to lunch, with a large canvas on which she had begun a painting of the house. In the afternoon she sat the children down and posed them for a portrait, after which she took from the attic an old folder of Chopin nocturnes and whacked away at the piano for two hours. This done, she brought in several armloads of flowers to adorn the house, her enthusiasm so running away with her that, in the end, there was even an enormous bouquet standing on the floor of the hall in a ten-gallon crock. At dinner she was gay. Afterward, instead of suggesting a game of two-handed pinochle as was her custom at the end of an exhausting day, she curled up in a chair with the second volume of *Lee's Lieutenants*, scarcely light reading, particularly since she had not read Volume One.

The next day was a duplicate of the first, with interesting variations. She undertook a portrait of me at my typewriter, but was scarcely started when something caught her eye out the window. She departed at once, leaving her paints and easel. At noon she was highly excited. By extending here and there the brick wall Willie Moss had built, by replanting a couple of magnolia trees, and moving nineteen boxwood bushes, she could finally have her little flower garden just off the back porch. That afternoon, along with Chopin, there was a seedsman's catalogue on the piano rack. Never before was Chopin strewn with so many flowers. That night Margaret undertook a water color of me while I read a book. Evidently I am a poor subject for portraiture; she did not complete the job.

This diligent activity continued all week. Serious discussions with high I.Q. friends now engrossed her. We had three dinner parties. She stacked the reading table with books from the public library, chiefly concerned with the history of Virginia and its famous sons and daughters. A tuner came from Richmond to repair the piano. Several neighbors called, separately, to give expert opinion on Margaret's horticultural project. She ordered a garden tractor, and sixty dollars worth of seeds and shrubs. She completed the portraits of the children. Finally she rode her artistic hobby to a fall when she invaded the kitchen to do a pastel of the cook, who promptly quit.

Margaret added the culinary labor to her enthusiasms without a word of complaint. She even sharpened my dull carving knife, and at this point I began to take more interest in her new life. Here was tangible result. The children got in her way a bit, but the book said a woman must not let her offspring dominate her life, and she followed the book. One day, while Margaret was in Washington seeing an art exhibit, Lampert asked me suddenly, "Daddy, what's the matter with Mommy?"

"Oh," I said, mindful at that moment that lately I had become the nursemaid, "she has a fever."

His eyes were large and very round. "Will she die?" he inquired.

"Oh, no," I replied. "Nothing like that. She'll be better in a few days."

The children and I watched for signs of convalescence. The first came that night. Arriving home about dinnertime, Margaret was reminded by lack of activity in the kitchen that she had undertaken the cooking. We had hamburger sandwiches at a roadside stand. The children loved it. They thought it was a picnic and that Mommy was paying attention to them again.

The next day the lid blew off the pressure cooker. It was, in a way, symbolic. Margaret had planned a one-dish dinner to save time while she undertook a landscape in oil from the front porch after her piano practice. Her painting did not go well, perhaps because the children were helping her. She decided that her trees were wrong, and consulted a colored print of a famous Corot. His trees were better than hers, so she altered hers accordingly. Now the remainder of her canvas was wrong; what it needed, for composition, was Corot's road. She put in the road, which unbalanced her perspective, so she added Corot's mountains. Soon she had appropriated Corot's man on horseback, though on her canvas he was so small that she put him in a red coat for visibility. Corot's horse was going away, and this rump-side view bothered Margaret exceedingly. She solved the difficulty by giving the horse a very large white tail. At that point the pressure cooker on the kitchen stove exploded. Lampert put his foot through the new canvas in the excitement of the moment and Laurie sat down on the mixing palette and then, as in offset printing, transferred this impression to a red silk sofa in the living room. Margaret was still in the kitchen scrubbing our dinner from the floor and walls when the doorbell rang. The nurseryman had arrived with a truckload of shrubs that must be planted immediately.

That night the children and I had another picnic at the hamburger stand, but Margaret was not with us. She had gone to bed.

CHAPTER TWENTY-ONE

THE next morning I took a breakfast tray to Margaret after feeding the children and sending them outdoors. Clearly, she was in need of a bit of coddling, and nothing makes Margaret feel quite so pampered as breakfast in bed.

There was no surprise in my entrance. Women have an instinct for their husbands' lapses into sentimentality. She was sitting up in bed, smiling happily, about her shoulders a silk jacket I had not seen since our honeymoon. The eggs were overcooked, but Margaret said she liked them that way. She invited me to sit down on the bed beside her while she enjoyed this ultimate in feminine luxury.

"Recovered?" I asked cautiously.

"Oh yes," she said, as though with relief that her ordeal in intellectualism had now ended. She chuckled self-consciously. "Was I awfully silly?"

"Not at all," I said. "Perfectly normal."

She did not know whether this was a compliment or not, but gave me the benefit of the doubt, in gratitude for my unusual attentiveness. I poured her a cup of coffee.

"No demitasse," I said.

She looked down at the cup, slowly lifted it and drank thoughtfully.

"Are we as bad as Ned said we were?" she asked.

"We're not bad at all," I said.

"Are you sure?"

"Emphatically. I've been thinking about it."

"Then what upset me so much?"

"The fact that we've been coasting," I said. "We needed a holiday. Now we're rested, as you proved by breaking out as you did. I'm getting restless, too."

I pointed out that on the farm we are careful to mow the pastures in June and August to prevent the weeds from going to seed. Perhaps now the time had come for us to mow our mental weeds and put ourselves back into production.

"But Ned seems to think we can't accomplish anything here in the country."

"Do you believe that?" I asked.

Margaret cited the impact made upon us by the fresh air children, and by our editor friend, as examples that raised the issue of whether we were sitting on the sidelines, watching the world go by.

"We are not part of anything important," she concluded. "We are not one with anything heroic."

"Of course we are," I said. "We are as inseparable from the whole world as is the city man. Our vote is as important as any other. If this country goes down, we go with it. No one is any longer free from world impacts. Provincialism, like the limitations of space and time, is gone forever. Even here on the farm we specialize; we raise only beef. We are dependent on the baker for our bread."

I elaborated on this, pointing out that everyone is too dependent on the common welfare, too interdependent with world agony, to live a life apart. No one knows where the world is taking him, therefore the world has become every man's burden. As a result, country isolation is no more possible for the individual than is political isolation for a nation.

"But what do we contribute in a positive way?"

"I write about what I believe. I lecture concerning my convictions. We raise food, that the city man may eat. You are raising two children to be decent, democratic citizens. What more does the city man contribute than that? What more does our theatrical friend Basil contribute, for all his feverish running around, or the parents of Brownie and Angela in their Brooklyn environment, or Ned Sears in his ivory tower? They are more disturbed by the mass impacts of the city, perhaps, but they don't accomplish any more."

"But we're not growing," Margaret persisted. "As you said a moment ago, we're coasting. We are becoming mental hillbillies. The next thing you know we'll be going to cowboy movies on Saturday night."

"I like cowboy movies," I said, "I took the kids to one the other day. Lots of . . ."

"You see!" Margaret exclaimed.

"All right," I said. "But we don't want to blow the lid off the pressure cooker every day."

"That's unkind. You're avoiding the issue."

"So I am," I admitted. "We've worked for three years —and they've been hard years—to organize a leisurely life. I don't think we should get eager-beaver now and destroy what we have created. We just haven't learned how to make use of what we have."

"We're not going about it the right way."

"That we can change. We can read more; play less pinochle and solitaire. I can write and lecture more. We can mingle more with other people. We can get away from the farm now and then, to restore our perspective. It is merely a matter of putting first things first. We have organized the farm and our existence. Now let's organize our minds."

"What is our aim in life?"

"To be happy and useful."

Margaret thought that over for a moment. Then she said, "When I was in college I took a sociology course under J. O. Hertzler. He pointed out that people never reach their goal because they keep revising their objective. It's like a ship that gets almost to Southampton before the captain discovers he really wants to go to Oslo. Perhaps it's time we changed our course again."

"All right," I said. "But maybe we'd better take a bearing and find out where we are before we decide where to go. Maybe we're not even on the right boat."

But we were. For here on the farm we received, from deep in the ground, the nourishment without which our hearts would shrivel and die. Here also was a standard of living much higher than the city offered for the same money, the abundant quantities of wholesome food produced by the farm, the health engendered by outdoor life and hearty exercise. Here was quiet, if not peace; a happy childhood for our children; a sanctuary removed from the treadmill of urban life; friendship that had nothing to sell, though much to give; simplicity of living that tended to reduce complexities to workable solutions; and, above all, the daily reminder in all of nature that life had infinite meaning and purposeful direction.

Of all these, the last had become increasingly important to us, not so much for itself as for the corollary that sprang from it. Life has become too complex for man to master. No one can possibly absorb all the implications of modern existence. Individual decision is now the product of sorting, rejecting, and selecting from a vast mountain of possibilities. This requires perspective, for which modern society has set up no mechanics. Contemplation, once an art and a boon to everyone, has been crowded into the cells of the monastic orders, out of reach of most of us. As a substitute, we rely now on our commercial thinkers: newspaper columnists, radio commentators, and book writers, who, in the fever of daily competition, have even less time for contemplation than we have ourselves. The conflicting impacts of all these thinkers induce a schizophrenia which paralyzes our will to make decisions for ourselves.

In the country, however, Margaret and I have time to think. And we are close to nature, which tends to simplify, rather than complicate, the thought process. Out of our reflection has emerged a faith in the future of mankind which now is strong and durable.

Take one simple illustration. Fear of atomic destruction has become almost a national neurosis, despoiling adults of security and depriving young people of confidence in the future. Here on the farm, we cannot become overwhelmed by this fear. We tend to consider this phenomenon the product of a lack of faith, and therefore to be remediable. I can well imagine my preacher father's reaction, were he still living, to the threat of atomic destruction. He might have been thrown off stride momentarily by the heinousness of mankind which would loose, for destructive purposes, a power within which there is inherent so much good. But he would have seen the good shining through, and been reassured for tomorrow. He would have remembered that man quavered at the invention of gunpowder, dynamite, and poison gas, and had risen above them all. Then, faith unshaken, he would have gone out to adjure men to rise above self-destruction once again.

In the city I almost lost that faith into which I was born. Now in the country, which has whittled me down to my proper size and released in me the power to adjust myself to my limitations, I find myself recapturing the old faith. The planned order of the universe is visible in each change of season, in the birth of every calf, in the seed-scattering industry of the squirrels, the pollinating activity of the honey bees, the rebuilding of worn-out soil by nature even without the help of man, and of course, in the optimism of little children. Nature's activity works unceasingly toward the creation of a better future. The impetus always pushes ahead. Surely, if there is so much hope for the natural world, that power in the universe which we call God must have some equally hopeful future in store for man, who is part of nature. Surely He will not let man destroy himself; the natural world is a contradiction of such a premise.

This faith, born of rural living, gives us serenity and hope. It is the product of too much struggle to be jeopardized by a removal from the environment that has produced it. And, added to the other credits in the ledger of rural life, it produces a trial balance strongly in favor of continued country living.

"All right," Margaret said when we had reached this conclusion, "that settles that."

"Yes," I agreed. "What we must do now is to arrange our lives so that we will not tumble into the obvious pitfalls. Let's correct those deficiencies which are correctable. We still won't have perfection, but our lives should be in reasonable balance."

"For the moment," said Margaret logically. She smiled.

"You know," she burst out excitedly, "what we really need is a little apartment in New York, rented the year round, to which we could go whenever we start losing our perspective. I could get away from the children, and you could talk to editors and read in the libraries. We'd keep sharp, don't you think?"

Here was an enthusiasm that required immediate chilling.

"Who's going to pay the rent?" I asked.

Practical aspects have never influenced Margaret.

"We rarely go to New York because hotels are such a nuisance," she said. "Really, I'm serious about this."

So was I.

"Look, darling," I said. "You know us very well. When we moved to the country, you didn't get back to town for four years. If we took an apartment in New York it would be four years before we got back here—and by that time this place would be in such disrepair we'd have all our work to do over again."

"God forbid," Margaret said, and she meant it devoutly.